The Making of the Twentieth Century

This new series of specially commissioned titles focuses attention on significant and often controversial events and themes of world history this century. The authors, many of them already outstanding in their field, have tried to close the gap between the intelligent layman, whose interest is aroused by recent history, and the specialist student at university. Each book will therefore provide sufficient narrative and explanation for the newcomer while offering the specialist student detailed source-references and bibliographies, together with interpretation and reassessment in the light of recent scholarship.

In the choice of subjects there will be a balance between breadth in some spheres and detail in others; between the essentially political and matters scientific, economic or social. The series cannot be a comprehensive account of everything that has happened in the twentieth century, but it will provide a guide to recent research and explain something of the times of extraordinary change and complexity in which we live.

The Making of the Twentieth Century

Series Editor: CHRISTOPHER THORNE

Other titles in the Series include

Already published

In preparation

Britain and France in the Middle East and North Africa, 1914-1967

Ann Williams

Macmillan

London · Melbourne · Toronto

St Martin's Press

New York

1 9 6 8

Published by
MACMILLAN AND CO LTD
Little Essex Street London WC2
and also at Bombay Calcutta and Madras
Macmillan South Africa (Publishers) Pty Ltd Johannesburg
The Macmillan Company of Australia Pty Ltd Melbourne
The Macmillan Company of Canada Ltd Toronto
St Martin's Press Inc New York

Library of Congress catalog card no. 68–26561

Printed in Great Britain by
ROBERT MACLEHOSE AND CO LTD
The University Press, Glasgow

Contents

Plates and Maps

PLATES

between pages 146 and 147

The author and publishers wish to thank the following for permission to reproduce the plates: 5 (*lower*), Associated Press; 1b, British Museum; 8 (*lower*), André Debatty from *Le 13 Mai et la Presse* (published by Armand Colin); 2a, Mr C. J. Edmonds; (*upper*), Imperial War Museum; 4b, Iraq Petroleum Company; 6 (*lower*), 7 (*top left*), Keystone; 1a, 2b and c, 3, 4a, 6(*upper*), 7 (*top and bottom right*), The Radio Times Hulton Picture Library; 8 (*upper*), Tunisian Embassy.

The cartoon on page 108 is by Pol Ferjac and originally appeared in *Le Canard Enchaîné*.

MAPS

ACKNOWLEDGEMENTS

The author and publishers wish to thank the following for permission to reproduce the maps:

Maps 1 and 3: Messrs Chatto & Windus, based on a map in E. Monroe, *Britain's Moment in the Middle East*.

Map 2: Khayat's, Beirut, based on a map in Zeine N. Zeine, *The Struggle for Arab Independence*.

Preface

THE scope of this book is indicated by its title, but even within these limits it is necessarily selective in its material. It is hoped that the Bibliography will enable those interested to follow up the political history of individual countries, and also social and economic changes in the Middle East and North Africa in the present century.

The transliteration of Arabic, Turkish and Persian personal names and place-names has, as always, given rise to many problems. As many of the people mentioned are familiar to newspaper readers in certain guises, for example, Nasser and Bourguiba, I have thought it best to leave them like this, but have in the process produced an untidy mixture of French and English transliteration.

I thank my mother for typing the manuscript. I should also like to thank the Librarian, and Miss Myrtle Matthews and the counter staff of King's College Library, Aberdeen; the Librarian of St Antony's Middle East Centre; the Librarian and staff of the School of Oriental and African Studies; the Librarian and staff of Chatham House Library; and also the Librarian and staff of the London Library for their kindness in providing books. The dedication of the book is an inadequate return for the help and friendship of Elizabeth Monroe.

Abbreviations

D.B.F.P. i	*Documents on British Foreign Policy*, series i
D.I.A. 1956	R.I.I.A., *Documents on International Affairs 1956*, ed. Noble Frankland (London, 1959)
Hurewitz, ii	J. C. Hurewitz, *Diplomacy in the Near and Middle East*, vol. ii, *1914–1956* (Princeton, 1956)
Julien	Ch.-A. Julien, *L'Afrique du Nord en marche*, 2nd ed. (Paris, 1953)
Le Tourneau	Roger Le Tourneau, *L'Évolution politique de L'Afrique du Nord Musulmane* (Paris, 1962)
Monroe	Elizabeth Monroe, *Britain's Moment in the Middle East* (London, 1963)

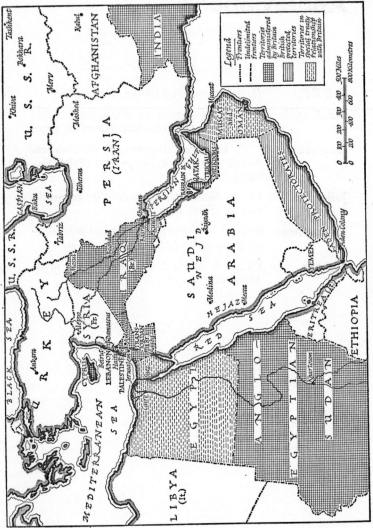

The Middle East — 1926

Introduction
The Middle East, the Maghrib and the West

THE term 'Middle East' came into common use at the beginning of the twentieth century,* and from the first it denoted
a sphere of Western political influence rather than a precise
geographical or ethnic area. At its widest extent it is held to
include the region from Turkey and the Mediterranean
seaboard lands to Jordan, Iraq and Iran in the east, the
Arabian peninsula in the south, with Egypt and Sudan on
the African continent. North Africa – the Maghrib – is
more compact geographically, bounded by the Sahara in
the south and the Mediterranean on the north. Its name,
'the island of the west', the 'jazirat al-maghrib', is the
traditional name given by the Arab geographers. Modern
North Africa contains the States of Libya, Tunisia, Algeria
and Morocco.

The whole of this area had been overrun by the Arab
invaders at the time of the great conquests of the seventh to
the eleventh centuries A.D. They had fought in the name of
their religion, Islam, which was based on the teachings and
traditions of the Prophet Muhammad and the divinely
revealed scripture of the Koran. Islam provided a system of
government as well as a faith. The Caliph, or deputy of the
Prophet, was the ruler and the Sharia, or Holy Law, was its
guiding code.

Islam was adopted by the Ottoman Turks who in the
fourteenth century overran Anatolia. They were warlike
tribes who had been converted in the frontier lands of

* It was invented in 1902 by the American historian A. T. Mahan.

Central Asia, and consequently their faith was a militant one. These warriors gradually overcame the Eastern Roman or Byzantine Empire and established themselves on both sides of the Bosporus. In 1453 the city of Constantinople fell to them, and from there they extended their rule by land to Egypt and further along the coast of North Africa, by sea to the islands of Greece, which gave them bases to harry the shipping of the West. Under Suleyman the Magnificent (1520–66) the Ottoman Empire reached its greatest extent. This indefatigable sultan led his armies as far as Persia in the East, where he met the opposition of the newly united Safavid Empire. In the West he extended Ottoman rule to the Balkans, but his failure to reach Vienna was prophetic of the later attempts and failures of the Ottomans.

The Ottoman sultan built a strongly centralised State. He was an absolute ruler and all his officials from the Grand Vizier down were technically his slaves. Most of the palace officials were recruited from the tribute of Christian boys levied every few years in the provinces. They were brought up as Muslims and trained for administrative posts or for the sultan's special body of troops, the janissaries. The Sublime Porte, originally the name of the Grand Vizier's residence and then of the administrative departments housed within it, was the name by which the Ottoman Government was known to the European powers.

Foreign communities were permitted to live within the Empire under their own laws and customs. These 'millets' existed right up to the end of the Empire and provided an important focus for nationalist discontent in the nineteenth century.

Other important concessions granted to foreigners were the Capitulations. The French first obtained these valuable trading rights from Suleyman the Magnificent in 1535, and their example was followed by the British in 1553. The Capitulations exempted the foreigners from Ottoman taxes and gave more extensive trading privileges to them than to the Ottoman himself. At first the system encouraged trade, but as the number of foreigners increased and the strength of the central Ottoman authority declined, the Capitulations became a symbol of humiliation within the Empire.

When the challenge of expanding its frontiers was removed the Empire began its slow decay. The long tentacles of the Constantinople bureaucracy could no longer hold its provinces together and it was threatened both from without and within. The diplomatic problem of the 'Eastern Question' began. This has been defined at its widest as 'the problem of filling up the vacuum created by the gradual recession of the Ottoman Empire from the frontiers it reached at the height of its expansion'.[1] Austria and Russia were deeply interested in what happened to the Balkan provinces. Russia hoped for an outlet to the warm waters of the Mediterranean and could push forward her claim as the champion of Orthodox Christianity in the Levant. Britain and France were anxious not to allow this because of the balance of power in Europe and because of their own growing interests in the Mediterranean. Their joint action in the Crimea in the 1850s showed their determination to keep Russia in her place.

Britain was already by this stage a 'great naval, Indian and colonial power'.[2] The Government of India was a powerful lobby in the forming of policy decisions. Of these the need to protect communications to India was the most important. The long route round the Cape had to be freed from Arab pirates of the Gulf and the threat of other Western rivals. Napoleon's scheme which began with the invasion of Egypt in 1798 was to stretch eastwards and threaten the whole of England's eastern trade. The latter part of the enterprise was never carried out, but it proved to Britain that she had to safeguard her possessions. In 1798 she made a treaty with the Sultan of Muscat, the first of a series of agreements with the Rulers of southern Arabia and the Gulf. Her policy of supporting Turkey was continued in the Arabian peninsula to prevent encroachments by Egypt. Her failure to strengthen Turkish rule there led to the occupation of Aden in 1839.

But Egypt itself was the linchpin of Britain's defence of India even before the Suez Canal was constructed. The short route to India, by ship to Alexandria and then over-land to Suez or the Persian Gulf, had much to recommend it, forty days' travel compared with five months round the Cape.[3] Britain joined the Ottomans in expelling the Napoleonic armies from the Nile, but the country did not remain subdued for long. Muhammad Ali, an Albanian soldier, seized control, was recognised as Viceroy of Egypt by the Sultan in 1805 and began a career of conquest which led into the Sudan, southern Arabia and back to Syria and the gates of Istanbul itself. Neither Britain nor France felt they could allow this blow at the Sultanate so they inter-vened to confine Muhammad Ali to Egypt and the Sudan. His subsequent reliance on French help did not please Britain who again felt that her interests were threatened.

The two Western powers co-operated over the project of the Canal at Suez. Britain was at first doubtful of the idea because she feared it would mean too much international competition and the taking on of greater burdens of defence. But Disraeli's large purchase of Canal shares meant a direct government involvement in the enterprise. In 1869 the Canal opened, and seven years later Britain and France had to assume Dual Control to ensure the working of the Canal and to support Egypt's collapsing economy. Neither power was anxious for colonial control. When Disraeli committed the British Government by buying the Canal shares there was an outcry from the Liberals at home against the assumption of any more responsibilities. France gradually took less and less part in the administra-tion of Egypt even though her bond-holders were heavily involved financially.

There was growing coldness between Britain and France in the last decade of the century. The Franco-Russian *rapprochement* of 1894 roused all the old feelings of menace from the Eastern powers. Attempts to insist on reform of the Ottoman Empire and to keep it intact seemed fruitless. The Congress of Berlin had done nothing to prevent continual upheaval in the Balkans. To encourage Russia appeared to upset the balance of Europe.

France was also interesting herself in Africa and in particular the headwaters of the Nile where Britain, through Egypt's claim to Sudan, was involved. The incident at Fashoda in 1898 caused bitter feeling between the two powers. Britain also feared that the French might hinder the scheme for a Cape-to-Cairo railway. But Britain herself was soon to realise that Germany was a greater danger than Russia and in 1907 she concluded an agreement with Russia on spheres of interest in Persia, which was valuable both for the defence of India and for its promise of oil.

France's role in the eastern Mediterranean was a less precise one; although romantics like Lamartine saw Syria as 'an admirable French colony waiting for France', most of his fellow countrymen were prepared to stress only their 'civilising mission'. René Ristelhueber's book *Les Traditions françaises au Liban*, published in the 1920s, presented the classic picture of French links with the Levant from the time of the Crusades. They had become the protectors of Catholicism including the Maronites and the Greek Catholics in the Ottoman Empire. Schools were established, charities endowed by the religious orders particularly by the Jesuits. The University of St Joseph in Beirut was founded in 1875 and with it an important Catholic printing-press. The French language became the common intellectual currency from Istanbul to Cairo. French newspapers and books were distributed widely among the reading public.

French investment was also important within the Ottoman Empire. On the eve of the First World War France held 60 per cent of its Debt compared with the 21 per cent held by Germany and 14 per cent by Britain.[4] French capital had played a large part in developing road and rail communications in Syria. Ports and municipal enterprises like gas and electricity had been supported. France had a controlling share in the Imperial Ottoman Bank and ran the *Régie des Tabacs*. The silk industry established in Lebanon and other industrial developments were promoted by French businessmen.

In North Africa France became more involved as a Mediterranean power. Charles X made a bid for prestige for the restored Bourbons in the invasion of Algeria in 1830. The prevalent French colonial theory of 'assimilation' still held sway and newly conquered lands were added to the departmental system of the mother country. Opinion in France was still very strongly against any colonial commitments. The country was underpopulated so that there was no pressing need for settlement colonies, nor did economic factors push her into colonisation. It was not until the European humiliations of 1870 that nationalism became more belligerent, but even then it was the colonials and the diplomats who urged France to increase her empire, rather than the Paris government. The exception was the two brief premierships of Jules Ferry in 1880–1 and 1883–5 which saw a considerable increase of France's possessions overseas. Her Mediterranean empire was extended by the protectorate over Tunisia confirmed by treaty in 1881, to buttress Algeria and combat Italy. Ferry felt that France was being overtaken by England and Germany in the new scramble for colonies. The idea of 'association', that is the protection of the mother country but the maintainance of native institutions, had gained ground and Tunisia kept her Bey.

France's aspirations were encouraged at the Congress

of Berlin in 1878 by Bismarck, who wanted to divert her attention from the loss of Alsace–Lorraine. In Tunisia as in Algeria economic motives for intervention were not convincing. The one place in North Africa where France had serious financial commitments was Egypt, and there she seemed content to let Britain gain more political influence, realising that, as Professor Lori of Bordeaux commented: 'We are no longer strong enough in Egypt to exercise real control, but we are still in a position to hamper the English.'[5] The colonial party which had developed in France at the end of the century under Eugène Étienne saw the advantage of Egypt as a bargaining-pawn. The two powers haggled over Morocco, which France wanted to consolidate her North African possessions, in return for Great Britain's freer hand in Egypt. The horse-trading was concluded by the Entente of 1904. France declared that she would not 'obstruct the action of Great Britain in that country by asking that a limit of time be fixed for the British occupation or in any other manner . . .'.

In return France obtained a protectorate over Morocco except for the region of Spanish influence on the Atlantic coast. The Entente also linked the two powers in loose and unaccustomed bonds of friendship which were to be put to the test in 1914.

NOTES TO INTRODUCTION

1. Sir Reader Bullard (ed.), *The Middle East: A Political and Economic Survey*, 3rd ed. (London, 1958), p. 8.
2. Quoted in Lord Hankey, *The Supreme Command, 1914–1918* (London, 1961), vol. i, p. 46.
3. Z. Y. Hershlag, *Introduction to the Modern Economic History of the Middle East* (Leiden, 1964), pp. 89–90.
4. Hershlag, op. cit. p. 65.
5. J. J. Mathews, 'Egypt and the Formation of the Anglo-French Entente 1904' (thesis, Philadelphia, 1939), p. 63.

1 Problems in War and Peace

THE First World War drew both Britain and France more closely into the affairs of the Middle East. On the outbreak of war the Allies hoped for the neutrality of the Turks so that they would not be involved with a Mediterranean front. Neither power, however, made any effort to win over the hesitant empire. A secret alliance between Turkey and Germany predisposed the Turks towards joining the Central Powers, and British tactlessness encouraged the pro-Germans to press their argument home. Two ships, paid for by public subscription in Turkey and still in the yards in Britain, were seized by the British Government. Germany immediately made capital out of the incident by sending two cruisers, the *Goeben* and the *Breslau*, already in the Mediterranean, to serve as substitutes for the Turkish Navy. At the end of October these ships joined in the bombardment of the Russian Black Sea ports and the Allies declared war on Turkey.

Great Britain was the power most affected by the extension of the war. Her interests in Egypt, still under the suzerainty of Turkey, led her to declare a protectorate over the country in December 1914.* Two pressure groups, the Government of India and the Admiralty, urged an invasion in the Persian Gulf. The former was worried about the defence of routes to India, the latter about the supply of oil they hoped would flow from the fields of southern Persia. The Government of India, ruler of many Muslims,

* The reasons for this particular arrangement are discussed in Chapter 3. There will be a further book in this series, on the Ottoman Empire and its successors.

was also apprehensive about the Straits and the possibility of so great a Muslim centre as Constantinople in hostile hands. Lloyd George in his *War Memoirs* stressed the importance of the area:

The Turkish Empire lay across the track by land or water to our great possessions in the East. . . . It was vital for our communications, for our prestige in the East that once the Turks declared war against us, we should defeat and discredit them without loss of time. The importance of a speedy victory over the Turks for the security of the British Empire was undeniable.[1]

So the British military effort in the area was divided. The heavy Turko-German offensive in Palestine and Sinai in 1914 and the beginning of 1915 kept a considerable section of the available British forces tied to Egypt. In Mesopotamia the invasion of the Tigris and Euphrates went slowly, and although the primary aim of keeping the oil supply open was achieved, the further attempt to secure the area by taking Baghdad was not. The loss of Kut el-Amara on 29 April 1916 and the capture of General Townshend marked the lowest ebb of fortune on this front.

The Middle East in both war and peace was only a 'side-show', and was to be seen against the background of First World War strategy and diplomacy. None the less it occupied the attention of the War Cabinet, and in particular of Lord Kitchener, who hoped that his Egyptian tour of duty would not long be interrupted by hostilities. He made several suggestions for landings which would immobilise Turkey quickly, and so force her to peace terms. It was Winston Churchill's plan, however, which won the day. He suggested a naval bombardment of the Straits and Constantinople, followed by a military landing in the Gallipoli peninsula. Recent writings on the campaign and its leaders have explained the reasons for the disaster. The expedition was planned too quickly, little was known of the terrain, and supplies were unsuitable and inadequate from the beginning. Also the element of surprise was lost because the first attempt was made by the bombardment of naval forts in the Dardanelles. The withdrawal of troops in January 1916 after months of hardship ended any hope of a speedy reduction of the Turkish Empire.

While British soldiers were battling rather fruitlessly against the Turks, Western diplomats were assuming the death of the Turkish Empire and were planning its obsequies. In the first years of the war Britain and France were not the only powers involved. Russia, in particular, was a member of the Entente and her demands, the result of her long-standing interest in an outlet for her Black Sea fleet, had to be met. The first partition was worked out in diplomatic exchanges in March and April 1915, and the area was divided into zones of influence. The Russian Foreign Minister at once staked his claim: 'Toute solution serait insuffisante et précaire si la ville de Constantinople, la rive occidentale du Bosphore, de la mer de Marmora et des Dardenelles, ainsi que le Thrace méridionale jusqu'à la ligne Enos-Midia, n'étaient désormais incorporées à l'Empire Russe.'[2]

Poincaré and Grey, the French and British Foreign Ministers, were both worried by this demand, but were unable to protest because of their own ambitions. It was clear even at this early stage that France wanted Syria, and that for the French, Syria included Palestine and Cilicia.[3] They felt that this was owed them as a counter-balance to increased British power in Egypt. A second secret agreement was concluded in London in April 1915 between the Entente Powers and Italy, in order to bring the latter into the Allies' camp. Her rights to the Dodecanese islands, which she already occupied, were recognised, as well as her claim to a just share of the Mediterranean region adjacent to the province of Adalia, where Italy 'has already acquired rights and interests'.[4]

British demands in the area were clarified by the de

Allied plans for the partition of the Ottoman Empire:
Sykes–Picot Agreement, 1916

Bunsen Committee which met in April 1915. This gathering of representatives from various ministries, Foreign Office, War Office, India Office, Admiralty and the Board of Trade, under the chairmanship of Sir Maurice de Bunsen of the Foreign Office, met to discuss proposals for the settlement of the Middle East. The chief British concerns of the period were dominated by interests in India; the Muslim Holy Places must remain in Muslim hands, and the passage to India must be safeguarded by a British presence in the Persian Gulf and on both sides of the Suez Canal. Concerning the east bank of the Canal, the Committee vouchsafed that Palestine was to fall within the British sphere, but it made the reservation that 'Palestine must be recognised as a country whose destiny must be the subject of special negotiations, in which both belligerents and neutrals are alike interested'.[5]

The British Government was also in favour of supporting the Arabs, and in particular, the Sharif of Mecca, the Amir Hussein. Its aim seems to have been an anxiety to show itself in sympathy with the Islamic movement because of the large number of Muslims in the Indian army, rather than to encourage a revolt against Turkish rule. Kitchener was anxious to ensure that commitments to France with regard to Syria were not compromised. Sir Ronald Storrs, the Oriental Secretary at Cairo, was sent to the Sharif to see if an agreement would be welcome. Sir Henry McMahon, High Commissioner in Egypt, began a correspondence with the Sharif on 14 July 1915 which continued until the following January.[6] Britain was to recognise Arab independence with certain reservations; on the grounds that they were largely Christian the areas west of Damascus, Homs, Hama and Aleppo, were excluded, a clause which caused much difficulty later because it omitted to mention Palestine. Simultaneously, however, Britain was negotiating on this subject with her ally, France. France's representative, M. Picot, was told the gist of these arrangements at the time: 'M. Picot informed Sir Arthur Nicolson that, after great difficulties, he had obtained permission from his Government to agree to the towns of Aleppo, Hama, Homs and Damascus being included in the Arab dominions to be administered by the Arabs under French influence.'[7]

The refusal to promise Hussein lands which Britain's ally France claimed led to discussions between Grey and Cambon on the exact demands of the French. In November 1915 Sir Mark Sykes met M. Georges Picot to work out the detailed terms of a settlement. Sykes must have seen the Hussein–McMahon correspondence in Cairo, but he obviously did not consider it a binding arrangement, as the Sykes–Picot agreement drawn up in April 1916 differs from it in several respects.[8] It was based on the old idea of spheres of influence (see map on p. 12). France was to have an area from Damascus to Mosul. Great Britain was to control one from Gaza to Kirkuk, regions where they could establish 'such direct or indirect administration or control as they desire and as they may think fit to arrange with the Arab State or Confederation of Arab States'. A 'brown' area of the map, Palestine, was to be administered internationally, 'the form of which is to be decided upon after consultation with Russia, and subsequently with the other Allies, and the representative of the Shereef of Mecca'.

Where the McMahon letter had left things in the air, Sykes–Picot made a definite commitment. There was undoubtedly ambiguity in the two documents, but the Sharif seems to have been aware that Palestine was excluded, if not at the time then certainly in 1917 when the position was explained to him by the Arab Bureau in Cairo. It was only after Zionist arrivals had begun to reveal political ambitions, and after the Sharif's son, Feisal, had been turned out of Damascus in 1920, that a grievance based on McMahon's imprecision became a major issue between the Arabs and Britain.[9] In fact the McMahon agreement was not the only one to be made with an Arab leader in the course of the war. The Government of India sent Captain Shakespear, and after his death, Sir Percy Cox, to negotiate with Ibn Saud, the Wahabi leader of Arabia and the bitter rival of the Emir Hussein.

All these agreements had in common was the belief that the Western powers must take the place of the Turks when the Turkish Empire collapsed. Except in the deserts of Arabia none of them envisaged an independent Arab State without benefit of either French or British advice. These paternal arrangements were shaken by the events of 1916 and more especially of 1917. In June 1916 the Arab Revolt broke out; Hussein with British financial and military help raised the Arab tribes and began to move his warriors northwards, later to join up with Allenby's forces in the final defeat of the Turks in 1918.*

Criticism in Britain of the management of the war brought Lloyd George to the premiership at the end of 1916. Horrified by the slaughter on the Somme, he was more convinced than Asquith had been of the value of sideshows. His support led to a change of fortunes in the area. In June 1917 General Allenby was appointed Commander-in-Chief of the Egyptian Expeditionary Force and in the course of 1917 and 1918 he fought his way into possession of Palestine and Syria with the support of the Arabs. These years also saw an improvement in the British position in Mesopotamia, where Baghdad was taken in March 1917.

The last of the old style 'spheres of influence' treaties was drawn up by Britain, France and Italy in the spring of 1917 at St-Jean-de-Maurienne. It clarified the earlier treaty with Italy. Italy laid claim to a larger share of Asia Minor, and Palestine was again declared to be subject to international negotiation. But the situation was already changing

* Modern research has tended to minimise the part played by T. E. Lawrence, but the legend and the criticisms of it can be followed in the Bibliography.

rapidly. The United States came into the war in April 1917. The President and his adviser, Colonel House, told of the secret agreements for the partition of the Turkish Empire, were openly critical. The American Ambassador Morgenthau's special mission in 1917 and the later King–Crane Commission showed that America's intention was to pay more heed to the wishes of the peoples involved. In March 1917 the Tsarist régime was overthrown and the Bolsheviks repudiated the treaties of their predecessors. They also announced the provisions of the Sykes–Picot agreement to an attentive Arab world, and outraged the Arab leaders.

The same month saw the British Cabinet statement of its support for Jewish Zionist aspirations. The Zionist movement as a political force had arisen out of the pogroms of Russia and Eastern Europe in the nineteenth century. Under the early leadership of Theodore Herzl, whose book, *The Jewish State*, had a profound influence, international Zionist Congresses were inaugurated. The cause had been greeted with interest in Britain from the first, and in 1902 Joseph Chamberlain suggested that the Zionists should accept land for the Jewish Settlement in the East African Protectorate as an alternative to Palestine.[10] The idea was unacceptable to most Jews because of the importance they attached to the City of David, Jerusalem. The second stage of British political involvement with Zionism began after Chaim Weizmann took up an appointment in Chemistry at Manchester University, and became prominent in British Zionist circles. His friendship with C. P. Scott, the editor of the *Manchester Guardian*, who found him 'extraordinarily interesting – a rare combination of idealism and the severely practical which are the two essentials of statesmanship',[11] and his own charm and skill in negotiation brought his support of the Palestine Jewish State to the attention of the British Cabinet.[12]

The discussions on the issue were protracted, but on

2 November 1917 the Balfour Declaration was published. The statement said that 'His Majesty's Government view with favour the establishment in Palestine of a national home for the Jewish people and will use their best endeavours to facilitate the achievement of this object, it being clearly understood that nothing shall be done which may prejudice the civil and religious rights and political status enjoyed by Jews in any other country.' Leonard Stein's book *The Balfour Declaration* is a masterly analysis of the threads that went to make this tapestry, a compromise between the Zionist claims for the whole of Palestine and British liberal sympathy for an oppressed people. From the British point of view this benevolence was to be disastrous. Recent research has shown that conflicts between the two communities were already apparent, but no practical surveys were carried out before the Declaration was made.[13]

In January 1918 President Wilson announced his Fourteen Points which gave encouragement to the Arabs' aspirations for independence. Britain and France did not want to be left behind in this bid for goodwill. The Hogarth message stated that 'the Entente Powers were determined that the Arab race should be given full opportunity of once again forming a nation in the world. This could only be achieved by the Arabs themselves uniting, and Great Britain and her allies would pursue a policy with this ultimate unity in view.'[14] Six months later in reply to the inquiry of a Syrian group in Cairo, the British Government made the Declaration to the Seven, which said that in the areas of Arabia which were free before the war and the areas emancipated from Turkish control by the Arabs during the war, 'His Majesty's Government recognise the complete and sovereign independence of the Arabs'.[15] On 8 November Britain and France made a joint declaration of their intentions, and promised 'to encourage and assist in the establishment of indigenous Governments and Administrations in Syria and Mesopotamia'.

Whatever justification there might have been for ambiguous promises in 1916, two years later they were less excusable. The British Government had limited its freedom of action by engagements with the Arabs and the Jews, and had acted with a happy disregard of their undertakings with their French allies. The military set-backs of the early part of the war in Sinai had convinced the British that Palestine in friendly hands was essential for the safety of the Suez Canal with all that it implied for the defence of India. As Balfour said in a Memorandum in September 1919, it brought 'into clear relief what I fear is the unhappy truth, namely, that France, England and America have got themselves into a position over the Syrian problem so inextricably confused that no really neat and satisfactory issue is now possible for any of them.'[16]

The situation was aggravated by tension between Lloyd George and Clemenceau. The armistice with the Turks signed at Mudros in October 1918 brought a conflict between the Allies over supreme command of their fleet. On 15 October Lloyd George wrote caustically to Clemenceau:

'We have taken by far the larger part of the burden of war against Turkey in the Dardanelles and in Gallipoli, in Egypt, in Mesopotamia and in Palestine. . . . I do not see how I could possibly justify to the people of the British Empire that at the moment when the final attack upon Turkey was to be delivered, the command of Naval Forces which are overwhelmingly British, in a theatre of war associated with some of the most desperate and heroic fighting by troops from nearly every part of the British Empire should be handed over to a French Admiral. . . .'[17]

Turkey's surrender was technically to the Entente, but in fact to the British so that in all the areas in which France was interested the British were in charge at the time fighting stopped.

The rift did not widen at once. Lloyd George had preliminary talks with Clemenceau in London before the Peace

Conference met at Versailles. The discussions were based on the Sykes–Picot agreement. France hoped for concessions on the Rhine, so Clemenceau was prepared to ask the British Prime Minister what modifications he wanted in the terms. 'He replied "Mosul". I said "You shall have it. Anything else.?" He replied "Palestine". Again I said, "You shall have it".' He left London as he said 'somewhat doubtful as to the reception this arrangement would have in France, but well assured that to Great Britain at least it would prove satisfactory.'[18] When the Conference met at Versailles two main problems existed in the Middle East. A peace treaty had to be concluded with Turkey and a settlement had to be arranged for the Arab provinces of the former Ottoman Empire.

The first question was ostensibly settled by the Treaty of Sèvres in August 1920[19] but was disrupted by the nationalist movement of Mustafa Kemal in Turkey. This young officer had made his reputation in the First World War, particularly in the defence of Gallipoli, but his experiences had also taught him to despise the constitutional government in Turkey and to mistrust foreign intervention in Turkish affairs.[20] The Allies were alarmed at his continuing civil war after the Mudros armistice, and they supported the Greek Prime Minister, Venizelos, in his claim to the Greek Orthodox areas of western Anatolia, partly to keep Kemal in check. Kemal's firmness of purpose, based on the Turkish National Pact which clearly defined his intention to build a modern Turkish State, united the Turks behind him. The Turks played on this tension between Britain and France and managed to sign a formal treaty with France, which agreed to withdraw her troops, and also to accept a Syrian-Turkish frontier south of the one drawn at Sèvres, in return for economic concessions.[21]

Kemal's continued success in the latter part of 1921 and 1922 decimated the Greek army and led the British to prepare an ultimatum to the Turks. The general in

B

command at the Straits, General Harington, did not present it, but instead secured an armistice. The alarm that such a remote quarrel might have led Britain into war was one of the causes of Lloyd George's fall from power in 1922. The bargaining of Curzon and Ismet Pasha at Lausanne produced a new treaty in 1923.[22] This agreement, the most solid achievement of the post-war peace settlements, gave both sides what they wanted. The new nationalist government was recognised and the Supplementary Régime of the Straits ensured an open passage through the Straits for international shipping.

The Arab question was more complex. Lloyd George seized upon the joint declaration of 8 November 1918, saying that its intention was to supersede all earlier agreements, particularly that reached by Sykes–Picot. The British Government was now convinced that French ambitions in the Levant were dangerous and likely to provoke another war. It had also been persuaded that Arab nationalism was worthy of encouragement. The French, on the other hand, did not want the earlier decisions abandoned completely even if they agreed to some concessions to the British. They still felt that the whole Syrian region needed paternal guidance, and that if an Arab kingdom were established Britain would step in as its protector, depriving France of old ties that were her due. They wanted the same privileges in Syria as Britain was claiming in Mesopotamia.

The Council of Four met on 20 March 1919 to discuss the Syrian question. The upshot of their discussion was a compromise with the French, and a betrayal of what the Arabs had taken to be promises of full independence. Lloyd George felt bound to maintain that Great Britain had no claims on Syria for herself. President Wilson thought that agreement might be better reached by sending out a Commission to inquire what the wishes of the people in the regions were. Lloyd George agreed to the idea, but Clemenceau objected. Finally an American group, the King–Crane commission, went out unaccompanied by representatives from the other Allied powers. Its members reported that the Syrians were completely opposed to the idea of a French mandate. The French press meanwhile was stirring up a campaign of hatred against Britain which caused a sharp diplomatic exchange between the two governments.[23]

In September 1919 Lloyd George changed his tactics to get a quicker solution to the problem. British troops, he assured the French, would be removed from Cilicia and Syria at once. The Emir Feisal should be left in command of Damascus and the other towns allotted to him in the Sykes–Picot agreement. France should control Lebanon. Meanwhile the British Government urged Feisal to put his claim to the Council personally. Curzon wrote:

I urged Feisal to go to Paris unaccompanied by any Englishman and with no evidence of British inspiration or backing to see Clemenceau personally; to put before him his own position with clearness, cogency and moderation; to realise that this was in probability the last opportunity of coming to a friendly agreement with the French; that in the interests of all parties concerned, Arabs, French and British such an agreement was supremely desirable.[24]

Feisal was out of his element at Versailles, and apart from inspiring passages of flowery prose in the memoirs of those who saw him, his presence had little effect. Clemenceau had won the round.

NOTES TO CHAPTER I

1. D. Lloyd George, *War Memoirs* (London 1933–6), vol. iv, pp. 1802–3.
2. *D.B.F.P.* i. iv, p. 635.
3. Hurewitz, ii, pp. 9–10.
4. *D.B.F.P.* i. iv, p. 638.
5. Monroe, pp. 29–30.

6. British White Paper, Cmd. 5957.
7. *D.B.F.P.* i. iv, p. 481.
8. Ibid. pp. 245–7.
9. Monroe, p. 35.
10. Leonard Stein, *The Balfour Declaration* (London, 1961), pp. 3–4.
11. Quoted in ibid. p. 132.
12. The story that he received the promises of the Balfour Declaration in return for his scientific war work have recently been discounted; see Stein, op. cit. pp. 119–20.
13. Neville Mandel, 'Turks, Arabs and Jewish immigration into Palestine, 1882–1914', in *St Antony's Papers*, Middle Eastern Affairs, 4 (Oxford, 1965), pp. 77–108.
14. Hurewitz, ii, p. 29.
15. Ibid.
16. *D.B.F.P.* i. iv, p. 342.
17. H. H. Cumming, *Franco-British Rivalry in the Post-War Near East* (London, 1938), p. 55.
18. *D.B.F.P.* i. iv, pp. 340–1.
19. Hurewitz, ii, pp. 81–9.
20. See Lord Kinross, *Atatürk: The Rebirth of a Nation* (London, 1964).
21. Roderic H. Davison, *Turkish Diplomacy from Mudros to Lausanne* (in Gordon A. Craig and Felix Gilbert (ed.), *The Diplomats, 1919–1939* (Princeton and New York, 1963), Atheneum ed.), vol. 1, p. 189.
22. Hurewitz, ii, pp. 119–27.
23. *D.B.F.P.* i. iv, p. 318.
24. Ibid. p. 475.

2 International Trustee-
ship in the Levant

THE Versailles Conference broke up without settling the Arab problem. Its successor met in San Remo in 1920 to discuss the setting up of mandates, and among them a system of international control for the Arab provinces of the Ottoman Empire. Article 22 of the Covenant of the League of Nations, which established the system, was deliberately vague. It was said that President Wilson 'did not want a lawyer's treaty', and, in any case, the differences among the territories to be administered made a too rigid definition impossible. Section 4, dealing with 'certain communities formerly belonging to the Turkish Empire', declared that they had 'reached a stage of development where their existence as independent nations can be provisionally recognised subject to the rendering of administrative advice and assistance by a Mandatory, until such time as they are able to stand alone.'

A Permanent Mandates Commission was constituted. It consisted of independent experts and not, like some of its successors, of representatives of governments. Biannual reports were to be sent to it for consideration. It could tender advice to the Mandatory and advise the Council of the League of Nations on matters concerning the Mandates. The new system had the advantage of appealing to wide sections of opinion in Western countries. It pleased the emerging left-wing groups, who regarded international action with favour, and also the right-wing upholders of traditional imperialism, who reckoned that Britain and France would lose nothing under the new system.[1]

BRITISH MANDATE IN PALESTINE

The conflicting promises to Arab and Jew tempered British policy in Palestine and local attitudes to the establishment of British control from the beginning. Even before the Mandate came into force on 1 July 1920 there were signs of disillusionment in both communities in the period of military rule.

The terms of the Mandate gave Britain full control over foreign, legislative and administrative and defence policy.[2] The Mandatory was bound 'so far as circumstances permit [to] encourage local autonomy' and to preserve freedom of conscience. Article 4 set up 'an appropriate Jewish Agency for the purpose of advising and co-operating with the Administrator of Palestine in such economic, social and other matters as may affect the establishment of the Jewish National Home and the interests of the Jewish population in Palestine.' No similar liaison body was considered necessary for the Arabs at first, and they later refused to form one. The Arab Executive selected by a Palestine Arab Congress was hardly comparable, and the number of Arab parties made it difficult to obtain a unanimous Arab point of view in the early years of the Mandate.

Sir Herbert Samuel, the first High Commissioner, had been an early supporter of a Jewish National Home in Palestine, and his appointment was welcomed by the Zionists. He hoped, however, to be acceptable to both groups, as he indicated to Ronald Storrs: 'You know my policy with regard to the non-Jewish population – not only to treat them with absolute justice and every consideration for their interests in matters relating to the establishment of the Jewish National home, but also to adopt active measures to promote their well-being.'[3] Jewish immigration began at once and, in spite of the reassurances given by the High Commissioner, the Arabs began to fear the loss of their lands and the ultimate establishment of a Jewish majority in Palestine. The Churchill Memorandum, published in 1922, was an attempt on the part of the Colonial Office to explain more fully what the Balfour Declaration had implied.[4] It reaffirmed that Palestine as a whole was not to be converted into a Jewish National home, only that such a home should be founded in Palestine. It also stressed that the British Government did not contemplate 'the disappearance or subordination of the Arab population, language or culture in Palestine'.

Although this Declaration was possibly little less ambiguous than anything that had gone before, and certainly did not please either side, it ushered in a period of calm. A sound administrative system was established to replace the chaos caused by the collapse of Ottoman rule. Lord Plumer, the second High Commissioner, had emerged from the recriminations of the First World War with his reputation intact; he was 'a sensitive man of wide sympathy' and 'looked on fairness as one of the highest ideals'.[5] A police force was raised, and Lord Plumer's authority was such that security forces were reduced, though this was done against the advice of the Mandate Commission. But as one observer commented: 'Lord Plumer's personality in the country was worth a battalion, and it was not sufficiently appreciated that, when he left the country, a battalion might be necessary to make up for him.'[6]

Meanwhile the question of Transjordan had to be settled. It was part of geographical Syria, and had been occupied by British and Arab forces at the end of the war. When Feisal became King of Damascus, it was taken over by his officials, and later when he became candidate for the Iraqi throne his elder brother, the Emir Abdullah, gate-crashed the province and adopted it as his own. Transjordan was included in the British Mandate for Palestine, but the Mandatory was given discretionary powers 'to postpone or withhold such provisions of the Mandate as he consider inapplicable to the existing local conditions'. A White Paper in 1922 excluded Transjordan from the areas open to Jewish settlement,[7] and in the spring of the following year Sir Herbert Samuel promised independence after a short trial period under British rule. In 1928 a treaty was signed with the Emir Abdullah giving the country its own government with British tutelage over foreign policy and finance. During the régime a succession of British officers, of whom the most famous was Glubb Pasha, organised the army and created the Arab Legion.

In Palestine matters were not going smoothly. In September 1928 an incident took place at the Wailing Wall in Jerusalem, in the Temple area that is sacred to both Arabs and Jews. Nearly a year later in August 1929 further demonstrations took place, and violent attacks were made by each community on the other. Arabs attacked Jewish hospitals and synagogues in Hebron, Jaffa and Haifa, and the Jews retaliated by destroying mosques in Jaffa and Jerusalem. 133 Jews were killed and 116 Arabs. The British administration was not unduly alarmed at the clash, and thought its mistake had been in cutting down the garrison.[8]

Nevertheless, an investigation was demanded in Britain, and the Shaw Report, published as a White Paper in April 1930 after inquiry into the causes of violence, stressed, as earlier reports had done, the anxiety felt by the Arabs at the risk of being outnumbered by Jewish immigrants.[9] Yet again it urged the British Government to make a clear statement of how they saw the development of Palestine. The Arabs regarded the report as a vote in their favour, and looked forward to a period of limitation of Jewish immigration and of economic stability as a result of new recommendations on land tenure. But the publication of an open letter from the Prime Minister, Ramsay MacDonald, to the Jewish leader, Chaim Weizmann, on 14 February 1931, confused the issue by its reassurance to the Jews. It is not clear whether his letter was meant to be a deliberate modification of British policy or whether, in an attempt to placate the Jewish section of the population, the Prime Minister changed the emphasis of earlier declarations on dual obligations.[10] Whatever the intention of his statement the Arabs regarded it as 'the black letter', while the Jews welcomed it as a promise of increased support for the future.

The incident marked the beginning of British loss of control, although retribution did not fall on them immediately. The period 1931-6 saw an improvement in the economy of the country.[11] Jewish capital from Europe increased prosperity and it was a prosperity in which the Arabs shared indirectly. An attempt was made to improve their position by stabilising land tenure, but Jewish immigration mounted, and from 1933 mounted rapidly. The Nazi onslaught that drove Jewish capital to the Middle East brought with it boatloads of illegal immigrants, refugees from Hitler's tyranny in Germany. The result, as Elizabeth Monroe has said, 'dispelled for good the British hope of muddling through in Palestine.'[12]

Arab opposition crystallised; arms were smuggled in from outside. The Mufti of Jerusalem, expelled from Palestine, was welcomed in Syria. In 1936 the Arabs tried unsuccessfully to organise a general strike, and then revolt broke out. Martial law was declared, and the British forces in Palestine were increased threefold to nearly 30,000 men. The strike was called off, but guerrilla warfare continued.

A fresh Commission under Lord Peel was sent to Palestine on 5 November 1937, and eight months later published its recommendations.[13] It attributed the disorders to two underlying causes: Arab hatred for the Jewish National Home, and the Arabs' desire for independence. Its solution to the problem was a new one, partition. 'Partition seems to offer at least a chance of ultimate peace. We can see none in any other plan.' The British Government were prepared to accept the idea, but the proposals did not meet with favour in any other quarter. The Arabs felt unable to accept the frontiers suggested; the Jews after a meeting of the Zionist Congress rejected the 'palliatives' offered by the Commissioners. The Permanent Mandates Commission was against the immediate creation of two independent states. On 16 September 1937, however, the Council of the League of Nations suggested that Great Britain should work out a number of schemes for partition. The Commission sent to explore the idea dismissed the partition possibility and suggested two states joined in an economic federation.

By this time the British Government felt that the partition plan was unworkable on financial grounds. They returned to the idea of an understanding between the Jews and the Arabs. Undoubtedly tension in Europe and Italy's ambitions in the Mediterranean area led to the desire for an immediate settlement of the affair. They suggested a conference of both parties to discuss a way out of the difficulties, and in Palestine itself the administration took a tough line to restore order. Military courts were set up to deal with terrorists, but the rebels had the sympathy of the civilian population, and even with a strengthened force the guerrilla war was impossible to contain.

In February 1939 the British Government summoned a Round Table Conference of Jews, Palestinian Arabs and Arabs from neighbouring states to London. No agreement was reached at the meeting, nor did the mediations of the Arab leaders gathered in Cairo produce results. On 17 May 1939 Britain published a White Paper containing her suggestions.[14] There was to be no partition, but an independent state within ten years. Jewish immigration up to 75,000 was to be allowed for five years and thereafter only if the Arabs consented to it.

The Jews felt that this was a complete betrayal of their cause by the British, while the Arabs were horrified at the number of immigrants suggested. The policy outlined was the last in a succession of confused statements on the role of Britain in Palestine. The Permanent Mandates Commission rejected the Paper as not being in accordance with the Mandate, and quoted Britain herself as saying that the Mandate could not be worked under the present system. War interrupted any further discussion. Inevitably the Jews, the enemies of Hitler, declared their loyalty to Britain during the war and Ben Gurion gave the Jews their battle cry, 'We shall fight this war as if there was no White Paper and we shall fight the White Paper as if there was no war'. The Arab response was less whole-hearted. The Mufti and his immediate supporters joined Germany, but the majority of Arabs were content to enjoy a respite from fighting and remained neutral.

THE FRENCH MANDATE IN SYRIA AND LEBANON

Geographical Syria covered the whole area from Taurus to Sinai and from the Mediterranean to the Syrian desert. The creation of the Mandates divided it into two political regions, the southern part Palestine, which was under British control, and the northern part under French control. The French again divided their share into smaller states of which political Syria was one. The name 'Syria' will be used in this last sense in this chapter.

Before the San Remo Conference met the Emir Feisal had returned to Damascus bitterly disappointed, as were all the Arabs, with the outcome of his visit. On 20 March 1920 a Congress of Syrian notables in Damascus offered Feisal the kingship of the whole of geographical Syria, which he accepted. The action was denounced by both the British and the French Governments. The French army, which had now replaced the British troops occupying the area, was strengthened under the command of General Gouraud, appointed as High Commissioner and Commander-in-Chief in the autumn of 1919. On 19 July 1920 he sent a letter to Feisal in which he demanded the recognition of the French Mandate and the replacement of

Feisal's army by French forces. Feisal accepted what was virtually an ultimatum, but his reply did not reach General Gouraud in time, so the French forces engaged the Arabs at Maisalun and entered Damascus on 25 July. Feisal was forced to leave; not until later was he chosen as ruler of the new kingdom of Iraq.

San Remo confirmed the French in their new inheritance. The terms of the Mandate charged the French 'with the duty of rendering administrative advice and assistance to the population'.[15] Article I committed the Mandatory to frame an organic law for Syria and Lebanon within three years.

This organic law shall be framed in agreement with the native authorities and shall take into account the rights, interests and wishes of all the population inhabiting the said territory. The Mandatory shall further enact measures to facilitate the progressive development of Syria and Lebanon as independent states. Pending the coming into effect of the organic law, the Government of Syria and Lebanon shall be conducted in accordance with the spirit of this Mandate.

The area over which the French administration had control was one of mixed population of uneven social and economic development. The Syrian territory was largely Sunni Muslim in religion, although there was a Shi'i minority group in one of its ports. Lebanon was much more complex. The majority of its inhabitants, up to the beginning of Mandatory rule, was Maronite Christian, but there were also Sunni Muslims, and another Muslim minority sect, the Druses, in south Lebanon. Much of the area that is now Lebanon had been an autonomous province within the Ottoman Empire from 1860 to the outbreak of the First World War, and had benefited from French investment and trade with Europe in this period. Socially the population varied from the sophisticated town-dweller of Beirut and Damascus to the tribal Druse family.

The French Government's view of the Mandate was expressed by Robert de Caix at a meeting of the Permanent Mandates Commission.[16]

The Mandate is a provisional system designed to enable populations which, politically speaking, are still minors to educate themselves so as to arrive one day at full self-government. . . . Consequently, the mandate system calls for a complete native organisation, but side by side with it an organisation of a tutelary nature, possessing the necessary authority to ensure the good government and progress of the country.

The French conception of a 'tutelary' institution was a highly organised bureaucracy which, as S. H. Longrigg wrote: 'forms a curious contrast to the scale of operation of the half-dozen British officials, who from the winter of 1920–1 onwards formed in Baghdad the office of High Commissioner for Iraq.'[17] At the head of this machinery was the High Commissioner, who was appointed by, and responsible to the Ministry of Foreign Affairs in Paris. He had a Secretary-General and a multiplicity of departments dealing with all the services of government. Control extended outside the capital too; *Services Spéciaux*, French officials in the districts, were widely disliked and accused of interfering unduly in local affairs.

The first task of the Mandatory was to impose law and order, so that the first High Commissioners were all generals of some standing, Gouraud, Weygand and Sarrail. Politically the French administration embarked on a policy of dividing and ruling. The size of Lebanon was increased and it became Greater Lebanon on 20 August 1920. The former Christian enclave was increased in size in a way that counterbalanced its inhabitants by the addition of Muslim areas. Greater Lebanon was ruled by a French official and an Advisory Council representative of the Lebanese but nominated by the High Commissioner.[18] On 5 December 1924 the State of Syria was proclaimed with

Damascus as its capital. A Representative Council was set up with power to elect a president, who, in his turn, could choose a cabinet of five ministers. French supervision over this government was strictly maintained. The Alawi, Shi'i Muslim minority area of Latakia was controlled directly by a French governor.[19]

It was a bitter disappointment to the provinces which had hoped to gain their independence from all foreign control after their part in the First World War. The brief rule of Feisal at Damascus was looked back on with longing throughout the period of the French Mandate. In 1925 a violent revolt broke out among the Syrian Druses and soon spread to the surrounding areas. The protest was the result of the tactless imposition of social reforms on a traditional society. The Druses and the neighbouring Syrian nationalists were heartened by the humiliating defeat of General Michaud in the early part of the revolt, and the pacification carried out by Henri de Jouvenel, the civilian governor who replaced General Sarrail in November 1925, had to take into account political protests. The Lebanese Assembly was allowed to draft a constitution and the Syrians to hold elections for a new Representative Council.

Henri de Jouvenel and his successor, Henri Ponsot, undertook to negotiate with Syria a treaty similar to the Anglo-Iraqi Treaty of 1922. In February 1928 elections for a Constituent Assembly were permitted and the harsh measures of censorship and of summary jurisdiction introduced during the revolt were lifted. The French and the Syrians could not, however, come to an agreement over the form of a treaty. In May 1930 the Constituent Assembly was dissolved and the High Commissioner imposed his own constitution. It combined most of the provisions demanded by the moderate nationalists but emphasised the strength of the French Mandate: 'So long as the international obligations of France in regard to Syria remain in force, any provisions of the present Constitution which are of a nature to effect those obligations will be applicable only under conditions to be determined by agreement between the French and Syrian governments.'[20]

In Lebanon, where the connection with France had always been strong, French difficulties were less serious. The Maronites still retained their sympathy for the French and the French High Commission could play on their hostility to the Muslims. The carefully balanced constitution had been weighed to give each community a share of offices proportionate to its members. The first decade of the Republic was occupied with the internal struggle between the parties of Bishara al-Khury and Émile Eddé. Here and also in Syria in the first decade of the Mandate, the nationalist groups, usually supporting a leader rather than a political programme, found it difficult to overcome their personal differences and to unite against the Mandatory. In Syria before the first treaty negotiations a similar pattern of disunity existed; groups, hardly parties, formed round popular leaders.

The French Mandatory scored by this uncertain opposition. The High Commissioner in the early thirties pushed forward an economic programme which silenced criticism for a few years. But this uneasy peace could not last; national parties were changing. A Syrian National Party led by Antun Saadah began specifically to preach Syrian nationalism and its support grew in strength after the imprisonment of its leaders in 1935. In Lebanon a youth movement known as the 'Phalanges Libanaises' encouraged the idea of independent Lebanon. Other groups such as the Communists had a more limited following, but all preached against the Mandate. Vociferous demands for independence began again in Syria. The local French administration was inclined to treat these political stirrings with harshness until word came from Paris that their views were to be considered.

In June 1936 a new Popular Front government, led by

Léon Blum, came to power in Paris and was sympathetic to the idea of Syrian independence. A treaty of friendship and alliance was drawn up defining the relationship of Syria and France. The spirit of the document was that the two Governments 'prendront toutes mesures utiles pour assurer, au jour de la cessation du mandat, le transfert au seul Gouvernement syrien, des droits et obligations résultant de tous traités, conventions et autres actes internationaux conclus, par le Gouvernement français, en ce qui concerne la Syrie ou en son nom.'[21] A similar arrangement was made between France and Lebanon. The treaties were to last for twenty-five years and could be renewed at the end of the period, Syria's by negotiation and Lebanon's almost automatically. The treaties were never signed; the Popular Front government fell and the High Commissioner became more repressive.

After the negotiation of frontiers in the post-war period the French mandated territories had established their boundaries with the Republic of Turkey. France was to work for Syria's membership of the League of Nations. The Sanjaq of Alexandretta, a frontier district, known to the Turks as Hatay, remained a bone of contention. It was administered by the French as a special area. The Turks claimed it because they maintained that the majority of its population was Turkish.[22] In February 1937 the League of Nations formed a committee to draw up a Statute and Fundamental Law for the province. Turkey was determined to add the province to the republic and was helped to do so by the imminence of the Second World War, and the desire of Hitler's enemies to placate her. In 1938 she saw the election of a Turkish majority in the Sanjaq, and a year later annexed it. Syria had made the issue a test of goodwill, and although the French probably did as much as was possible to retain Alexandretta, its loss marked a serious deterioration in the relations between the Mandatory and the Syrians.

The arrival of a new High Commissioner, Gabriel Puaux, in January 1939, and his broadcast speech stressing France's mission to the Levant, led to a fresh outbreak of violence. Neighbouring Palestine set examples to both sides. There were strikes against the French for failing to ratify the treaty. M. Puaux flew to Paris for consultations and, fortified by government authority, suspended the Syrian constitution in July. The international situation and the fear of anarchy in the Near East had persuaded the French administration that the mandated territories could not be entrusted to govern themselves.

By 1939 it was clear that both the British and French Mandates were working badly. Britain herself had said that she could no longer rule Palestine under the original terms. Lord Milner had pointed out one of the difficulties at the beginning. 'The mandated territories are to be under the supervision of the League of Nations. But actual authority in each of these territories will be exercised by one member of that League, or by some native ruler or rulers, guided and assisted by a member of that League. As it seems to me there will in a sense be a divided sovereignty.'[23] The Levant states had proved him right.

The arrangement had been particularly unhappy in this part of the former Ottoman Empire which already had some experience of autonomy, and looked to the Western Allies in the First World War to give it complete independence. Foreign rule, whether or not it was softened by the title of international mandate, was regarded with hostility.

The great failure of French rule was to win the approval and co-operation of the Syrian and the bulk of the Lebanese people. A large part of the population and especially of the more articulate elements in it, was from the beginning highly critical of French rule if not irreconcilably opposed to it; and criticism and opposition did not grow less with the passing of time.[24]

The burden of providing a National Home for the Jews also gave the British in Palestine an impossible political task from the first.

These political grievances obscured the achievements of the Mandatory régimes.[25] Both the French and the British did much to improve social conditions in their territories; for example hospitals were set up and doctors and nurses trained. Money from the home governments in London and Paris, as well as from private companies, was forthcoming for investment in economic projects like the development of communications. In Palestine an able and dedicated British civil administration carried out the day-to-day business of government, and a system of courts administered justice. The French record in the administration of Syria and Lebanon was less good. French officials were often corrupt and avaricious. The French, as was customary in their overseas territories, built up an elaborate educational system. All these measures could be, and were, regarded as foreign exploitation and gave ammunition to the growing nationalist movements.

The final blow to the Mandatory system was the failure of the League of Nations itself. The Permanent Mandates Commission consisted of able and dispassionate men, but they only met biannually, and they had no sanctions to enforce any criticisms they made of the Mandatories. The whole system was a new one, and every precedent had to be created. This fact inevitably gave Britain and France wide discretionary powers in their administration of the Mandates, and increased the local feeling that the scheme was just a cloak for imperialism. Salvador de Madariaga had called the mandates system, 'the worst fig-leaf in the whole show',[26] and by 1939 the new generation of Middle Eastern politicians was eager to tear off this flimsy disguise.

NOTES ON CHAPTER 2

1. Monroe, p. 73.
2. British White Paper, Cmd. 1785 (London, 1922).
3. Sir Ronald Storrs, *Orientations* (London, 1937), p. 458.
4. Christopher Sykes, *Crossroads to Israel* (London, 1965), pp. 76–97.
5. Sykes, op. cit. p. 106.
6. Norman Bentwich, *England in Palestine* (London, 1932), p. 149.
7. British White Paper, Cmd. 1785.
8. Monroe, p. 81.
9. Report of the Commission on the Palestine Disturbances of August, 1929. Cmd. 3530 (London, 1930).
10. E.S.C.O. Foundation, *Palestine: a Study of Jewish, Arab and British Policies* (vol. ii, New Haven, 1947), pp. 656–60.
11. Monroe, pp. 80–1.
12. Ibid. p. 85.
13. Palestine Royal Commission (The Peel Commission) Report. Cmd. 5479 (London, 1937).
14. British White Paper, Cmd. 6019 (London, 1939).
15. S. H. Longrigg, *Syria and Lebanon under French Mandate* (London, 1958), pp. 376–80.
16. Quoted in A. H. Hourani, *Syria and Lebanon: a Political Essay* (London, 1946), pp. 169–70.
17. Longrigg, op. cit. p. 115.
18. Hourani, op. cit. pp. 180–5.
19. Ibid. p. 194.
20. Ibid. appendix A, No. 2, pp. 314–16.
21. Richard D. Robinson, *The First Turkish Republic* (Harvard, 1963), pp. 173–4.
22. Hourani, op. cit. pp. 206–13.
23. Lord Milner's memorandum of 8 March 1919 quoted in R. Winks (ed.), *Historiography of the British Empire–Commonwealth* (Durham, N.C., 1966) p. 300.
24. Hourani, op. cit. p. 176.
25. Hourani, Longrigg, and E.S.C.O. Foundation volume on Palestine give details of the running of the mandated territories.
26. Monroe, p. 141.

3 British Interests in the Middle East

ALTHOUGH Britain had interests throughout the Middle East, she did not directly make a colonial settlement in any part of it. The seventy-five square miles of Aden, first acquired as a coaling-station, took on a new importance after the opening of the Suez Canal in 1869. It was administered casually from Bombay until 1932 when it was taken over by the India Imperial Government in New Delhi. Five years later, in 1937, it was transferred to the control of the Colonial Office in London as a Crown Colony. Apart from this colony, the relationships of Britain and the Middle East were guarded by special treaties of friendship, by protectorate, or in the years after the First World War, by mandate. Until the loss of India in 1947 British policy decisions were made in two quarters. The Government of India made its own decisions on the Indian Ocean area. It negotiated with the Sheikhs of the Gulf and with Aden, and kept a Resident in Lower Mesopotamia until 1932. The Colonial Office and the Foreign Office dealt with Mediterranean interests. Persia lay between them, until in 1860 there was an agreement to divide the staffing of posts. After the First World War a Middle East Committee was set up to co-ordinate thinking on policy. The Cairo Conference in 1921 was a result of its labours, but the experiment in co-ordination did not continue.

The aim of British policy in the area was, wherever possible, to protect her interests without assuming direct control, but this ambition was not always easy to achieve in practice. The British Government's relations with Egypt

were a case in point. Its attitude to the defence of India
and the importance attached to Egypt in British thinking
about the Indian Empire made the position of that country
of vital significance.[1] The Anglo-French Entente of 1904
had given a freer hand to Britain in her management of
Egyptian affairs. The Khedivial decree attached to this
document provided greater security for the Canal bond-
holders, and gave greater powers to Egypt's British advisers.
The years of Lord Cromer's paternal administration had
also introduced large numbers of British officials.[2] But the
technical position of Britain in Egypt was nevertheless a
difficult one. The country and its Khedive remained under
Ottoman suzerainty. Particular problems inevitably arose
when Turkey joined the Central Powers at the beginning
of the war. Should Egypt be annexed by the British as a
security step in protecting the Canal? The idea of direct
annexation was abandoned in favour of a Protectorate, a
word which had particularly humiliating overtones for the
Egyptians.[3]

The creation of a Protectorate assumed that foreign rule
was not to be permanent, and therefore the political
institutions of the country were retained. The government
of the Khedive and the system of law for the Egyptians
remained in force. But in the case of Egypt the administration of Lord Cromer had introduced new principles,
particularly in the sphere of finance. His Indian experience
had a deep influence on his policy in Egypt. 'Whatever the
country – whether India, Burma or Egypt – the recipe must
always be the same: attention to the laws of sound finance,
and in particular to the importance of low taxation,
efficient fiscal administration, careful expenditure on re-
munerative public works, the minimum interference in the
internal and external traffic of goods.'[4] He also believed
that Western ideas should be introduced slowly. 'The
Government may take the people to water, but it is impossible to make them drink at the fountain of Western

knowledge or to imbibe Western ideas of what is good for
their welfare unless they are reasonably disposed to do so.'[5]
Thus before the Protectorate was established in Egypt
the Egyptians had experience of British rule, and from
their contacts with both French and British ideas were
learning the art of political opposition to their foreign
overlords.

Developments during the war did not improve Anglo-
Egyptian relations. The country was occupied by large
numbers of British and Imperial troops, and the population suffered considerably from the requisitions of food and
supplies made for their support.[6] Although allegedly not
allowed to take part in the fighting, the Egyptians suffered
heavy losses in the Camel Corps which supported Allenby's
advance into Syria. A strong nationalist movement against
British rule arose under Saad Zaghlul.[7] The strength of this
feeling was underestimated by the British Government,
more preoccupied as it was with other affairs at the peace
conference.

The revolt of 1919, triggered-off by the arrest of Zaghlul,
brought the problem home to Lloyd George. He sent out a
successful general, Lord Allenby, to replace as High
Commissioner Sir Reginald Wingate, whom many reckoned
to be inclined to bow to nationalist demands.[8] Zaghlul
and his colleagues were immediately released from their
internment in Malta. Allenby's prompt action started the
administration working again, and London promised a
Mission, under Lord Milner, to look into the Egyptian
situation.[9] Rumour had it even before the Commission
arrived that the British would insist on the preservation of
the Protectorate, which caused more outbreaks of violence.
The recommendations of the Commission were, however,
sympathetic to the nationalists, although as Duff Cooper
later wrote in his memoirs, 'his [Lord Milner's] manner of
handling the affair in its final stages showed a strange lack
of technical skill'[10]. The Report said that the Protectorate

was to be abolished, but that British forces must be maintained in Egypt for the protection of imperial communications. Its second main recommendation was that Britain
should keep some measure of control over Egypt's internal
affairs in the interests of its largely foreign business community. The Sudan was not mentioned. The nationalists
had not been consulted, and they felt that the recommendations only amounted to the old protectorate in a new
guise.

In 1921 Curzon issued a Memorandum which promised
immediate abolition of the protectorate on the signature
of a treaty.[11] To the Egyptians this was not acceptable
because of the Sudan issue. Egypt had traditional claims to
the Sudan, claims which had been strengthened at the end
of the nineteenth century by disputes over the headwaters
of the Nile. Britain had stepped in to calm the Sudan after
the revolt of the Mahdi, and a Condominium was set up
whereby Britain and Egypt ruled the area conjointly, with
the expectation that it would be returned to Egypt when
she could rule it for herself. Sudan provided a happy
meeting-ground for the dedicated earnestness of British
administrators, who, finding the less sophisticated population easier to deal with than their more politically conscious neighbours, settled down to an administration of
peace and justice.[12] They also introduced economic
schemes, like the later scheme for growing cotton on a co-
operative basis in the Sudanese Gezira on land between the
rivers, which worked smoothly.[13] The problem with Egypt
arose over the control of Egyptian forces in the Sudan.
Curzon wanted them under the Governor-General in the
Sudan. Egypt could not accept this solution.

The deadlock was only broken by Allenby's determination to see the Protectorate abolished and his threat of
resignation if it were not. Known as 'The Bull', he was
extremely impatient at the slowness of London politicians
and himself went to England to force a result.

'Well,' he says to Lloyd George, 'it is no good disputing any longer. I have told you what I think is necessary. I have waited for five weeks for a decision, and I can't wait any longer: I shall tell Lady Allenby to come home.' He was, it seems, not mistaken in his view of the politicians: Lloyd George, hearing the ultimatum, rises and puts his hand on Allenby's arm. 'You have waited five weeks, Lord Allenby', he says, 'wait five minutes more.'[14]

The Declaration of February 1922 which Allenby obtained abolished the Protectorate, and on 1 March Egypt became an independent sovereign state, with the Sultan as king.[15] The British Government reserved the right to maintain troops to defend Egypt and the Canal, to protect foreign minorities and control the Sudan, 'until such time as it may be possible by discussion and friendly accommodation on both sides to conclude agreements in regard thereto between His Majesty's Government and the Government of Egypt.'

The terms were still not satisfactory for the nationalists, and Zaghlul Pasha, returned to power in new parliamentary elections, made further attempts to negotiate with the British Government with the Sudan as the main bargaining counter. Ramsay MacDonald, however, was clear that there could be 'no question of the British Government abandoning the Sudan until their work is done'. The situation was inflamed beyond all hope of saving by the murder of Sir Lee Stack on 19 November 1924 in a Cairo street. He was Governor-General of the Sudan and Sirdar, or Commander-in-Chief, of the Egyptian Army and was at the time the personal guest of Lord Allenby at the Residency. Horror at the death of his friend destroyed the High Commissioner's usual moderation and he sent a punitive note to the Egyptian Government. It demanded an immediate apology, punishment, and payment of an indemnity of £500,000 to Britain. All Egyptian troops were to be removed from the Sudan, and the Sudan was to have unlimited rights to draw on the Nile waters.[16] London considered that Allenby had gone too far in these measures, particularly the last, and he was recalled.

Zaghlul's party had no share in the murder and the politicians responsible for the plot were quickly arrested and sent for trial. The harm done to Anglo-Egyptian relations was deep. Lord Lloyd, Allenby's successor as High Commissioner, felt 'that good administration was the first requirement to be fulfilled and that all other questions were subordinate to it'. He was helped by the confusion of Egyptian politics. The independence of the country led to the emergence of the king as an element in the political situation, and there was no longer a united front among the nationalists. Zaghlul's Wafd party, the only one with nation-wide support, declined in prestige, and tentative negotiations were made in 1930 by the British with parties that were little more than personal followings, to settle outstanding problems, but they inevitably came to nothing.

But within the next five years several factors combined to bring the two countries to discuss their difficulties once again. The rise of Fascist Italy, established as Egypt's neighbour in Libya, brought the defence clauses of the 1922 Declaration to the fore, and Mussolini's Abyssinian ambitions increased Egyptian as well as British anxiety. In Egypt dislike of Britain persisted, but a greater dislike and fear of Italy drove Egypt's quarrelsome parties to unite.

The United Front presented a note to the High Commissioner, now Sir Miles Lampson, asking for treaty negotiations to be opened. The treaty signed in 1936 announced the end of British military occupation, but because the Suez Canal was vital as a means of communication, Britain was authorised 'to station forces in Egyptian territory in the vicinity of the Canal in the zone specified with a view to ensuring in co-operation with Egyptian forces the defence of the Canal'.[17]

It was recognised by both parties that the 'aim of their administration in the Sudan must be the welfare of the Sudanese', but although the 1899 arrangements were confirmed there was no longer any restriction on Egyptian immigration or commerce in the Sudan. The difficult question of Capitulations, the trading agreements granted by the Ottomans to foreign powers, which had been abolished in the rest of the former Ottoman Empire by the Lausanne Treaty of 1923, was deferred to a conference at Montreux where they were abolished. The Mixed Courts, in which foreigners had till then conducted all legislation, were to be run down gradually to give Egypt complete legal sovereignty in twelve years. Egypt's application for membership of the League of Nations was supported and she was admitted in May 1937. It looked as if a new era in Anglo-Egyptian relations might begin, but the concessions had been made too late to be of lasting value. Britain's Palestine policy had destroyed her reputation in the Middle East, and Egypt, persuaded by this as well as by the indignity of her own non-independence, determined to move away from British tutelage.

THE MANDATE FOR IRAQ

Iraq, as Mesopotamia became known, was, like Palestine, granted to Britain as a Mandate at the San Remo Conference. The vilayets of Baghdad and Basra were already in British hands as a result of the wartime campaigns. The question of Mosul still had to be decided, although as has already been seen, Clemenceau had given Lloyd George an assurance that Britain should have it. The political situation in Iraq as a whole was complicated by the existence of two strong minorities, the Kurds in the north and the Shi'i Muslims on the Euphrates, within a predominantly Sunni Muslim population.

The British Deputy Chief Political Officer in charge at

this time was Arnold (later Sir Arnold) Wilson, 'good-looking, able and intelligent, and extremely ambitious.'[18] He was in favour of paternal British administration and close links between Iraq and India. Efficient and rather high-handed, he had little time for Arab demands for a share in government. Delay in making a decision about the future of Iraq, followed by the declaration of the British Mandate which disappointed those who hoped for the complete independence of the country, led to revolts in 1920. Military reinforcements had to be brought from India to subdue the discontented regions.

Violent anti-British feeling was not long-lasting. Iraq feared the ambitions of the new Turkish régime on her northern frontier and accepted British rule as a preferable alternative to a return of the Turks. The pill was sugared too by the appointment of Sir Percy Cox in October 1920 to replace the unbending Sir Arnold Wilson. Sir Percy, perhaps one of the best administrators in the history of British imperialism, was known to be sympathetic to Arab national aspirations, and indicated from the beginning that he would mitigate mandatory rule by means of a treaty.[19]

Early in 1921 the India Office gave up its control of Iraq to the Colonial Office, then under the secretaryship of Winston Churchill. Churchill's conference summoned to Cairo a number of experts on Middle Eastern affairs.[20] In the matter of Iraq they suggested that Feisal, recently turned out of Damascus by the French, should be put forward for the throne of Iraq for which there was no obvious internal candidate. Britain still supported the Hashemite family, but because of its abandonment of the Sykes–Picot agreement on Palestine and on Mosul, did not feel able to stand up to the French action in Syria. A referendum was held in Iraq and on 23 August 1921 Feisal was crowned as king.[21]

The Cairo conference also recommended the reduction

of British forces in Iraq and announced that in 1922 the Royal Air Force would take over control of local security. Considerable improvements had already been made in communications in the war. The reorganisation of provincial government was begun, and although some difficulties arose, the co-operation of British advisers and local officials worked fairly smoothly. The High Commissioner had over-all authority but he worked from the first with a Council of Iraqi ministers selected from all religious groups, assisted by British advisers. The new King Feisal, a Sunni Muslim, trod warily through the religious problems of his new kingdom. His reign of twelve years and the continuity in British officialdom probably played a large part in making the régime acceptable to the Iraqis.

As soon as the new King was installed negotiations began for an Anglo-Iraqi Treaty. It was perhaps, as Longrigg has summed it up, 'unquestionably the most prudent and most imaginative way to handle a situation which lacked all precedent', but even this could not conceal for some the bitter medicine of mandatory control.[22] The treaty was concluded on 10 October 1922.[23] Britain promised to provide 'the State of Iraq with such advice and assistance as may be required during the period of the present Treaty, without prejudice to her national sovereignty'. Iraq was to have diplomatic representation in London, and she was to be put forward as a member of the League of Nations as soon as possible. Provision was made for con-stitutional development and there were to be financial and religious safeguards. No barrier was to stand in the way of Iraq joining any league of Arab States. The treaty was to last for twenty years, but could be revised within this period if necessary. (This was later modified to four years after the Turkish Treaty was signed in 1923.)

The question of Mosul still remained as a matter of uneasiness for the Iraqis, and a source of contention between them and their Turkish neighbours. The main point at issue seems, at the time, to have been British concern about a defensible northern frontier for a country so close to the passage to India. Britain wanted a frontier in the mountains to the north of Mosul, not in the plains to the south of it, although people were aware of the existence of oil. C. J. Edmonds, who was in Iraq throughout the inter-war period, wrote in his memoirs: 'Although the world Press was wont to represent the battle as part of a gigantic struggle for the control of oil, it is interesting to recall how very little oil figured in our calculations, at my level at any rate; I do not remember a single document in which oil was mentioned as a factor of outstanding importance.'[24] The League of Nations sent out a Commission to investigate the problem and its recommendations were that the northern province should be added to Basra and Baghdad. In December 1925 Mosul was awarded to Iraq. The success did a great deal to reconcile hesitant Iraqi opinion to British rule.

Iraq developed fairly well in the period after the First World War within the framework of a poor economy. The strength of her position as a communications link between east and west increased with the greater use of air and telegraph. Her relationships with other Arab countries were extended, and apart from occasional traditional border raids peace was maintained with her northern neighbour Turkey. Inside the country finance was put on a better footing, taxation reorganised and the National Debt reduced. On the other side of the balance sheet the minority groups, the Kurds and the Assyrians, still caused anxiety.[25] Parliamentary institutions had been introduced, but the constant changes of cabinet reveal that parliamentary government was not understood, and was not really very satisfactory.

By 1930 there was a strong demand for Iraq's right to govern herself with complete independence, and negotiations took place to end the Mandate. The treaty was finally signed in January 1931, and took the form of a preferential alliance between the two powers.[26] The Mandate was officially terminated. Arrangements were made by the British for the defence of Iraq, and Britain was allowed to keep the two air bases of Habbaniyah and Shaiba. She was also allowed to maintain forces in the area for a period of five years. Iraq was to house a British military mission and to be able to call upon British officials when in need of their services. The treaty was concluded before nationalist demands grew too bitter. In the thirties there were frequent demands for a complete break with Great Britain, but conservative politicians, among whom Nuri es-Said was already notable, maintained their insistence on friendly relations between the two governments.[27]

INLFUENCE BY TREATY

The post-First World War period added further problems for Britain in the region of Persia and the Gulf. The spheres-of-interest arrangement made with Russia in 1907 had been destroyed by the Bolshevik revolution and now there was fear of Communist expansion in northern Persia. Britain had a special interest in the region and was anxious to maintain a stable régime supported by the British. Curzon had a special soft spot for a country he knew well, and saw it as part of a scheme to extend British control from India to the Mediterranean. Sir Percy Cox was sent to negotiate with the Persian Prime Minister Vusuq'd-Daulah in August 1919.[28]

Iran (as Persia preferred to be called) was to receive 'at the cost of the Persian Government, the services of whatever expert advisers may, after consultation between the two governments, be considered necessary for the several departments of the Persian administration'. Military equipment and skilled officers were to help build a strong

Iranian army 'for the establishment and preservation of order in the country and on its frontiers'. The British Government offered a loan of £2,000,000 at a rate of 7 per cent interest to help with the creation of the army and the improvement of communications within the country. The agreement met with strong opposition from Iranian nationalists, and was also criticised by the United States and France who felt that Britain was arriving at too complete a control of Persian affairs. In May 1920 Russian troops invaded northern Iran, and Britain announced that she had no obligation to defend Iran; this assertion combined with international opposition killed the Treaty. The *coup d'état* of Reza Shah which brought a new régime to power in Iran, changed the course of events. He repudiated British help and Britain did not enter the scene again, except as the foreign power principally concerned in the production of Persian oil.

In the Gulf some nineteenth-century 'exclusive treaty' arrangements with the Sheikhs still held good. In Saudi Arabia a new ally, Ibn Saud, had been acquired during the war. His quarrel with the Emir Hussein led to his capture of Mecca in 1925; he also added the Hejaz to his patrimony. The Treaty of Jiddah signed between Britain and the King in May 1927 stressed 'the complete and absolute independence of the dominions of His Majesty the King of the Hejaz and Nejd and its Dependencies'.[29] In return Britain gave him her protection.

The importance of Aden as a port on the route to India has already been mentioned, and this fact accounted for the actual garrisoning of the town and its subsequent adoption as a Crown Colony. The area behind Aden was ignored by Britain until the First World War when the sudden descent of the Turks to within twenty miles of the port demonstrated its vulnerability. A convention with the Turks drew rough frontiers between the Yemen and the Aden Protectorate, the territories in the port's hinterland, and this agreement was confirmed by the 1934 Treaty of Sanaa between Britain and Yemen. Ambiguity about frontiers remained because the Arabic word *hudud* means both frontiers and area,[30] and provided a good excuse for Yemen to interfere in Adeni affairs in the 1960s. The chieftains of the Protectorate were gradually brought under control. Harold Ingrams 'was one of the most notable of those spearheads of the Pax Britannica for he virtually pacified the Eastern Protectorate single handed.'[31] In the years 1936 to 1939 he made agreements with more than 1300 local chieftains to create a general truce known as 'Ingram's Peace'. The treaties were modelled on those which had led to the formation of the Federation of Malay States.

Further east Britain had acquired responsibilities in the nineteenth century. The original name of the Trucial Coast, 'the pirate coast', explained the reason for intervention. No colony or protectorate was created and the states retained their own rulers, Muscat and Oman its Sultan, Kuwait and the smaller regions, like Abu Dhabi, Shahran and Bahrain, their Sheikhs. Originally the Government of India had supervisory powers in the region, and Lord Curzon visiting the Gulf in 1903 expressed British views on their relations with the Sheikhs.

Chiefs, of the relations that were thus created, and which by your own consent constituted the British Government the guardian of inter-tribal peace, there grew up political ties between the Government of India and yourselves, whereby the British Government became your overlords and protectors, and you have relations with no other power. . . . The British Government have no desire to interfere, and have never interfered in your internal affairs, provided that the Chiefs govern their territories with justice, and respect the rights of the foreign traders residing therein.[32]

Britain's representative was the Political Resident in Bahrain who had four Political Agents in Bahrain and

Qatar and two for the seven Trucial Sheikhdoms. He also had the support of the military advisers in the Persian Gulf and if need be, in Aden. The Resident's functions were difficult to define. He had no powers to advise the local rulers as had the British Agents in the Aden Protectorate. The 'special position' of Britain in the Gulf was chiefly concerned with piracy, foreign affairs and defence. The exclusive treaty rights symbolised what Britain felt was best in her relationship with the Arabs. She gained loyalty and indirect control without too much involvement, easy enough in desert circumstances, and before the Second World War avoided the weary bickerings of nationalist opposition.

OIL IN BRITISH POLICY

Oil interests had played some part in British wartime policy in Mesopotamia, and it may have been in the minds of some politicians when the negotiations for Mosul were taking place. But the first important developments in the post-war years took place in Iran. Oil had been discovered there in 1908, and Lord Curzon had it in mind when negotiating for the treaty in 1919. A British Cabinet memorandum of 9 August in the same year mentioned that 'we possess in the south-western corner of Persia great assets in the shape of the oilfields, which are worked for the British Navy and which give us a commanding interest in that part of the world.'[33]

The Shah of Persia had granted the first concession to William Knox D'Arcy in 1901. He was allowed to form a company for the exploitation of the oil resources in the whole country, except for the northern provinces, for a period of sixty years, in return for a payment to the Shah and a further 16 per cent of the annual net profits. It was some years before a commercial quantity of oil was found, but in 1909 the Anglo-Persian Oil Company came into

C   W.B.F.

being* and three years later a refinery was built on the island of Abadan. The use of petroleum was developing rapidly. The Navy had gone over to oil in 1912; motor cars and aeroplanes were creating an increasing demand for the new fuel. In July 1914 the British Government itself decided to purchase a controlling interest in the new Company.

After the war difficulties arose with the new régime in Iran concerning the validity of the concession and also over the right to exploit the northern provinces. Further problems for the Company were caused by the tribal Sheikhs of the southern provinces who could obstruct the flow of oil to the refinery at Abadan. The matter came to a head in 1932 when the Iranian Government cancelled the Company's privileges on the ground that 'The Anglo-Persian Oil Company has been repeatedly informed by Persian Government that the D'Arcy Concession of 1901 does not protect the interests of the Persian Government and that it is necessary to place relations between (the two) . . . on a new basis which will provide for the real interests of Persia.'[34]

The new agreement, which was ratified by the Iranian Majlis on 28 May 1933 reduced the geographical area of the concession.[35] The new royalty was to be four shillings a ton on all oil produced, to avoid the quibble over what the net profits were. The agreement was granted for a further period of sixty years from the date of signing the treaty, which took the concession to 1922. Both sides had made concessions and both gained in the new treaty, but the main cause for satisfaction was the era of peaceful relations which it heralded. The next five years saw increased production of oil and the expansion of the industry.

In Iraq the British Government had more competition from other powers. Three groups, one German, one

* It became the Anglo-Iranian Oil Company in 1935 and the British Petroleum Company in 1954.

British and one Anglo-Dutch, had been investigating the possibilities of oil in the area, and in 1914 they combined to reorganise the Turkish Petroleum Company founded two years earlier.[36] In March 1914, as a result of British Government persuasion, the Anglo-Persian Oil Company took a block of shares in the Turkish Company, thereby creating a British controlling interest. After the war, France, who had renounced what now appeared to be an important source of revenue in Mosul, asked for and obtained the 25 per cent share in the Company which had formerly been Germany's. The United States also felt that they should have a share in the oil discoveries, citing the 'Open Door' policy which they maintained throughout the Middle East.[37] Not until 1928 was the matter finally settled, at which date the four groups concerned agreed each to hold 23 per cent of the shares with a further 5 per cent for the American who had throughout handled the negotiations, Calouste Gulbenkian.[38]

On 14 March 1925 the Turkish Petroleum Company had been granted, except for the Basra zone, concessions for seventy-five years. Iraq's royalty was to be four shillings a ton on all oil produced. Three years later the 'Red Line' agreement was drawn up among the Companies concerned in the concession, prohibiting them from obtaining independent concessions within the Iraqi and Persian Gulf area. Further provisional concessions were granted to the Company (which became the Iraq Petroleum Company) in 1931. The industry developed extensively after this last agreement which provided for the building of a pipeline to carry the oil to a Mediterranean port. By 1934 two pipelines, one to Tripoli in Lebanon, the other to Haifa in Palestine, were working. Three years later a refinery was built at Haifa. The province of Basra was added to the concessionary territory in 1938.

THE BRITISH IN THE MIDDLE EAST

On the eve of the Second World War Britain looked at her position east of Suez with reasonable satisfaction. Her route to India was safeguarded. She had improved communications with her eastern empire. The unsettled areas of southern Arabia were peaceful under her protection. In Iraq the burdens of the Mandate had been set aside and goodwill maintained with the former mandated territory. Increasingly, too, oil was flowing to boost the external trade figures of the home country.

In no part of the Arab world had the British attempted to make colonial settlements as did the French in North Africa. The British served as soldiers and administrators. They worked within the traditional structure of government, and usually trained native officials to take responsibility under British guidance with the idea that they would take over when independence was granted. Sudan and Iraq were examples of this system. Many of the British officials, for instance Sir Percy Cox in Iraq, and Sir Reader Bullard in Persia, were deeply interested in the people they governed, and steeped in knowledge of their languages and culture.[39] It was possible for one man like Harold Ingrams to work, respected and with success, in an area where foreigners were virtually unknown. Another Englishman, Sir Charles Belgrave, although not a representative of the British Government, could answer an advertisement in the personal column of *The Times* to become adviser to the Sheikh of Bahrain, where he remained for thirty years, in which period he did a great deal to modernise the Sheikhdom.[40]

These gentlemanly relationships were possible with the older generation of Arabs, a ruling group who had more in common with the British than with the majority of their own people. In places like Egypt where a new generation of politicians was already taking over, the

British had a rougher ride even in the twenties and thirties. For the rest, Britain emerged from the Second World War in decline to find that she had few friends left in the Middle East, and that the benefits of security and good administration that she had granted were already forgotten.

NOTES TO CHAPTER 3

1. Ronald Robinson and John Gallagher, *Africa and the Victorians: the Official Mind of Imperialism* (London, 1961), pp. 155–9.
2. See Lord Cromer, *Modern Egypt* (2 vols., London, 1908).
3. Tom Little, *Egypt* (rev. ed. London, 1967), p. 125.
4. Roger Owen, 'The influence of Lord Cromer's Indian experience on British policy in Egypt, 1883–1907', in *St Antony's Papers*, Middle Eastern Affairs, 4 (Oxford, 1965), p. 113.
5. Quoted in ibid.
6. Jean and Simonne Lacouture, *Egypt in Transition* (Eng. ed., London, 1958), pp. 82–5.
7. Elie Kedourie, 'Sa'ad Zaghlul and the British', in *St Antony's Papers*, Middle Eastern Affairs, 2 (London, 1961), pp. 139–60.
8. Monroe, pp. 56–7.
9. British White Paper, Cmd. 1131 (London, 1922).
10. Duff Cooper, *Old Men Forget* (London, 1954), p. 102.
11. John Marlowe, *Anglo-Egyptian Relations, 1800–1953* (London, 1954), pp. 242–4.
12. See bibliography for books on administration of Sudan.
13. See Arthur Gaitskell, *Gezira: a Story of Development in the Sudan* (London, 1959).
14. A. Wavell, *Allenby in Egypt* (London, 1943), pp. 76–7.
15. Kedourie, op. cit. pp. 158–9.
16. Monroe, p. 76.
17. R.I.I.A., *Documents in International Affairs, 1936* (London, 1937), pp. 478–503.
18. Ronald Storrs, *Orientations* (London, 1937), p. 247. See John Marlowe, *Late Victorian: the biography of Sir Arnold Talbot Wilson* (London, 1967).

19. The day-to-day working of the British administration in Iraq can be followed in Gertrude Bell's *Letters* (see bibliography).
20. Monroe, p. 68.
21. S. H. Longrigg, *Iraq, 1900–1950* (London, 1953), pp. 130–3.
22. Ibid. p. 134.
23. Hurewitz, ii, p. 111.
24. C. J. Edmonds, *Kurds, Turks and Arabs: Politics, Travel and Research in North-Eastern Iraq, 1919–1925* (London, 1957), p. 398.
25. Longrigg, op. cit. pp. 191–200.
26. Hurewitz, ii, pp. 178–81.
27. See Lord Birdwood, *Nuri as-Said* (London, 1959).
28. Peter Avery, *Modern Iran* (London, 1965), p. 203.
29. Hurewitz, ii, pp. 149–50.
30. Harold Ingrams, *The Yemen* (London, 1963), p. 69.
31. David Holden, *Farewell to Arabia* (London, 1966), p. 37. See Harold Ingram's own account of his career in *Arabia and the Isles* (3rd ed., London, 1966).
32. Quoted in Holden, op. cit. p. 146.
33. *D.B.F.P.* i., pp. 1119–22.
34. Hurewitz, ii, p. 188.
35. Ibid. p. 188–96.
36. Hurewitz, i, pp. 276 ff.
37. Hurewitz, ii, p. 77.
38. B. Shwadran, *The Middle East, Oil and the Great Powers*, (2nd rev. ed., New York, 1959), pp. 244 ff.
39. Sir Reader Bullard, *The Camels Must Go* (London, 1951).
40. Sir Charles Belgrave, *Personal Column* (London, 1960).

4 The French in North Africa

By the outbreak of the First World War France's claim to her North African empire was unchallenged by other European powers. Her views on colonialism were being worked out on the assimilated lands of Algeria and in the protectorates of Tunisia and Morocco. Within the general framework of colonial theory institutions had to be developed and relationships established. No definite attempt was made to work out a pattern in advance. There was no single ministry directing policy in Paris. Algeria was in the charge of the Ministry of the Interior; Tunisia and Morocco under the Ministry of Foreign Affairs. Hardly any co-operation existed among the administrations of North Africa and little experience was gained from mistakes made in other areas. It was not until 1937 that a Haut-Comité Méditerranéan was set up, charged with the co-ordination of Muslim affairs. 'Pour la première fois', wrote its Chairman, Charles-André Julien, 'Algériens, Marocains et Tunisiens eurent la possibilité de s'expliquer librement devant les pouvoirs politiques.'[1] It did not survive for long.

The background to the affairs of North Africa between the wars was the instability of successive French governments. Few of them could afford to force through unpopular policies, as the failures of the Blum Popular Front in carrying out its North African and Middle Eastern policies showed. Reluctant at first to assume the burdens of colonial administration, the majority of the French people and their rulers in the twenties and thirties regarded France *d'outremer* with some pride. They were often complacent about France's 'civilising mission'. In North Africa itself the *colons* formed an *élite* in their own world; they had little or no contact with the Muslim section of the population. The Civil Service was largely French. As late as 1956, the Governor-General in Algeria announced that out of 864 appointments only eight Muslims had high administrative posts.[2] The same story could be told of the army. In 1958 the army in Algeria had one Algerian general (appointed that year) and 400 Algerian officers out of 30,000 officers commissioned. Algeria's experience was paralleled in Tunisia and Morocco.

ALGERIA

Although Algeria had been one of the three Ottoman regencies of North Africa, Turkish rule was never very effective. The country was difficult to hold even for the Turkish beys in Algiers. Its towns, of which Algiers was the most important, were seaports looking out into the Mediterranean. Communication with the interior was hazardous. The French, settling in the 1830s on the specious excuse of putting down the pirates, ran into difficulties from the first. They had no plan of conquest, nor particular economic gain after the initial seizure of the treasury.[3] The 1837 Treaty of Tafna gave the French a limited area of control in Algiers and the coastal towns, but the insecurity of this foothold soon became apparent. The revolt of Abd el-Kader in 1835 had been followed by the resistance of the Muslim brotherhoods. Kabylia, the home of Berber tribes, took longer to reduce but it was more or less brought under control by the end of the 1850s. This was not the end of opposition to French rule; a revolt took place in 1864, and a serious general rising provoked by famine, and France's defeat in the Franco-Prussian War, in 1871. The harsh reduction of the country after the latter rebellion subdued it, but at the cost of enormous Muslim and Berber loss of life.

While the military conquest was still being carried out the French began to settle Algeria. Muslim law covered three main kinds of land tenure. First came the *habus* lands, religious lands held in perpetuity, similar to the *waqf* lands of the Middle East. Secondly there was privately held land, *mulk*, and finally tribal property known in North Africa as '*arsh* lands. In the first years of the conquest the *habus* lands were distributed and also some private property where no title could be shown by the occupant. When General Bugeaud was appointed as Governor in 1841 he began to encourage systematic colonisation. The lands were given to army veterans, the first large-scale group of *colons*, and the growing of vines was encouraged. Official policy favoured the breaking down of the tribal system and in the early 1840s tribes were apportioned areas, in which they were to stay: the cantonment system. Bugeaud also began to break up the tribally held lands into individual holdings, a policy developed more fully in the Senatus-Consultus of 1863, which divided the tribes into villages and encouraged individuals to buy their own land. In France itself the advantage of settlement in Algeria was preached widely. *Colons* were offered stocked smallholdings as an inducement to go, and the army was employed in building roads and villages. After 1871 numbers of *colons* came from the lost provinces of Alsace and Lorraine.

The Second Empire saw a slight change in attitude to Algeria. Napoleon III liked to consider himself as Emperor of the Arabs, so emphasis was put on the Arabness of Algeria; he did little more than pay lip service to the idea, but none the less antagonised the *colons* who feared a loss of their privileges. The policy of assimilation was carried on steadily. In 1848 Algeria was made part of France and divided into three departments, Algiers, Oran and Constantine, similar to the departments of the mother country. Muslim Algerians were entitled to become French citizens under the Senatus-Consultus of 1865, that is if they renounced their status as Muslims, a particularly humiliating clause since five years later Jews were allowed to take up full French citizenship without any restrictive promises as a reward for their services in the Franco-Prussian War. In 1881 the Code de l'Indigénat was promulgated. It drew up a list of crimes and punishments applicable only to Muslims, such as criticising the French or the colonial government.

The final governmental decree of the nineteenth century regulating Algerian affairs came in 1896 when the three departments were put under the control of a Governor-General, chosen in Paris. The Ministry of the Interior supervised the setting up of a French system of education in the country. In Algeria the Governor-General could legislate by decree. A council called the Financial Delegations could give assent to the budget which the colonial government presented. The *colons* had a two-thirds majority in this assembly and their strength as a powerful pressure group in Paris on the subject of Algerian affairs was assisted by this financial control.

The political exhaustion of the country after the French conquest left it passive for several decades. The First World War did not touch North Africa physically, although Algerians worked in French factories and were conscripted for the army. One sheikh was quoted by the Constantine Arab Bureau as saying in 1914, 'On peut augmenter les impôts, nous prendre nos biens; mais nous ne donnerons pas nos enfants.'[4] Several protest revolts against the French took place in the provinces. Germany expressed some sympathy with the Muslim protest and in 1916 a committee for the independence of Algeria and Tunisia was set up in Berlin.[5] One of its members was a son of Abd el-Kader. Another malcontent, Moulay Hafid, gathered a group around him in Barcelona. The administration was not perturbed by fears of wide-spread unrest and Paris took Algeria's contribution to the war effort for granted. Two deputies, however, did try to get recognition for the part she had played. Georges Clemenceau and Georges Leygues wrote to the President of the Council, Aristide Briand, on 25 November 1915 speaking of the great loyalty and attachment of the Algerians to France.[6] They suggested a moderate programme of improvement: French citizenship without loss of Muslim status; increased native Algerian representation in both colonial and municipal elections; and a Higher Council in Paris to supervise Algerian affairs in which Algerians should take part. They also wanted a reform of Arab taxes and new guarantees of land tenure.

Only when Clemenceau himself became President was anything done, and then all but a few of his proposals were rejected. Arab taxation was investigated, and on 4 February 1919 a new electoral law was passed. This gave French citizenship to Algerians who were at least twenty-five years old, celibate or monogamous, who had never been convicted of a crime or an act of hostility towards the French. Additional requirements were that the prospective voter should be able to speak or write French, to have been in the armed services, or be a property owner of some standing. The law was little enough of a concession to the Muslims, particularly as the harsh Code de l'Indigénat made arrest on some trivial offence a common occurrence. It remained in force none the less until 1944, and was the constant target of attack by the nationalists as their protest grew stronger.

The *colon* section of the community regarded the law as a threat to their position, especially in the towns where they feared Muslim majorities might result. A gathering of mayors on 27 May 1920 asked for 'le retour à une politique indigène plus rationnelle et plus en rapport avec les exigences de la securité des populations de l'intérieur'.[7] They hoped to remove the Muslim element completely from local government by taking away its right to share in the election of mayors, and to limit Muslim representation on local councils considerably. They also asked for restoration of an earlier law giving strict disciplinary powers to the administration, which was immediately carried out. This law also remained on the statute books until 1944.

Opposition was roused by the legislation but it was uncertain and unorganised. The Emir Khaled, a grandson of Abd el-Kader, stood as candidate in the municipal elections with a programme opposing the disciplinary powers acquired by the administration and any form of extraordinary jurisdiction.[8] He asked for complete assimilation with the French citizens of Algeria. Indeed this was one of the cries of the early nationalist platform – that if there were to be assimilation it had not gone far enough. Khaled's election was declared null and void, but two years later he was found addressing the visiting President Millerand, demanding for Muslims the right 'prendre définitivement rang dans la grande famille française', and to give the Algerians parliamentary representation in France.[9] His petition had no effect.

The French Government hardened its imperial line in the last years of the twenties. Disturbances in Morocco were causing anxiety. In Algeria the Residency feared the growth of communism and some workers did join the party, but the most politically active group of Muslim Algerians at the time were in Paris, not in Algeria. Messali Hadj formed there a Workers' Party, the Étoile Nord-africaine, in 1926.[10] Maurice Viollette, Governor from 1925 to 1927, tried to get the Financial Delegations to carry out a social programme but failed in face of opposition from the *colons* who managed to get him recalled.[11] He had committed the serious error of relying on the Muslims rather than the *colons*. No Governor-General had done this before, and none was to risk it again. M. Régnier, Minister of the Interior, was sent out to inquire into the matter and his report supported the *colon* view. By 1930 it looked to the Europeans as though French policy had worked. The celebration for the centenary passed with many speeches of self-congratulation on the achievement.[12] The *colons*, many of whom were second and third generations, regarded their position as secure. They were Algeria. They had little or no contact with the fast-growing Muslim population. Only a few perceptive colonial administrators like Augustin Berque appreciated the lessons some Muslim Algerians were learning from their French education.

In 1935 the Popular Front government raised nationalist hopes as it had in Syria and Lebanon. Maurice Viollette from his experience as Governor-General realised that the initiative for reform had to come from Paris.[13] He felt that the Arab *élite* might feel frustrated because of their lack of political opportunity. The 'projet Blum–Viollette' which he introduced gave citizenship to certain Muslim Algerians without prejudicing their Sharia status. The *élite* were to be former soldiers, those with university degrees and officials in the administration. The failure to pass this Act was later seen as a turning point in Franco-Arab relations, but at the time Viollette's prophetic words and the lost opportunity passed unheeded amid the sound and fury of nations.

THE FRENCH PROTECTORATE IN TUNISIA AND MOROCCO

By the 1880s French colonial theorists had changed their views on the relationship of the mother country to its subject peoples. Jules Ferry, who was responsible for the acquisition of Tunisia, felt that a protectorate with the parallel local and French administrations existing side by side was to be preferred to the earlier assimilation practised in Algeria. Tunisia was in a different position from either Algeria or the later acquired Morocco because it had so much more consciousness as a 'state'. The Arab Hafsid dynasty who ruled the region from the thirteenth to the fifteenth centuries had forged it into a definite kingdom. The Ottoman beys who succeeded them kept a better control over their territory than their western neighbours were able to do, partly because it was less mountainous and easier to rule from coastal Tunis.

It was an area more open to influence from the West than the rest of the Maghrib. Liberal ideas took so great a hold that in 1856 a constitution was granted. The experiment was soon over, but it was a heartening gesture for later Tunisian nationalists to look back on. The beylical family, the Husainids, whose fortunes were founded in the early eighteenth century, remained till the end of the Protectorate. European interest in the area had already begun before the French arrived, the protection of investments in a shaky economy being the alleged reason for French intervention.[14] The possibility of Italian or British influence becoming too strong on the eastern borders of Algeria was probably a more forceful argument for a closer French relationship with Tunisia.

Two documents defined France's position within the country. The first, the Treaty of Kassar Said (often known as the Treaty of Bardo) was signed with the Bey Mohamed Sadoq on 13 May 1881. The French were to guarantee law and order and to conduct foreign affairs. There was to be a French Resident Minister who would act at the Bey's side, principally, in the beginning, to restore the country's financial equilibrium. These arrangements were augmented two years later by the Resident Minister Paul Cambon's Marsa Convention with the Bey (8 June 1883). Vaguely worded, it gave the French plenty of room for increasing their authority, because as a preamble to the financial clauses there was the general statement: 'A fin de faciliter au Gouvernement français l'accomplissement de son Protectorat, S.A. le Bey s'engage a procéder aux réformes administratives, judiciaires et financières que le Gouvernement français jugera utiles.'[15] No mention was made here of the limited duration of the Protectorate promised in the earlier treaty.

Tunisia was not, like Algeria, linked to the departments of metropolitan France, but within the country a system of French-style government departments called 'directions' was set up. These were largely in the hands of settler civil servants. The Muslim *qaid* remained in the local district but he too was watched by a French overseer, a *Contrôleur civil* after 1884. The next step was to make both the *qaids* and the tribal sheikhs civil servants and responsible to the administration.

The changeover of lands was not so harsh a process in Tunisia as elsewhere in the Maghrib. No large-scale military operations were necessary to reduce the country and this gave the French a better start than they had had in Algeria. European settlement had begun before 1881. A number of large companies like the Societé Marseillaise had bought great estates and were letting lands commercially. The *habus* lands were kept intact, but a scheme of renting them in perpetuity was evolved, known as the *enzel* right. After 1905 these lands could be sold. Thus although Tunisians lost many of their lands, the process was cushioned by the absence of violence and European settlement took a smaller proportion of the best cultivable lands than in Algeria, which made for a more peaceful relationship in the first years of the Protectorate.

It was soon apparent that French administration and French education were taking hold, and in Tunisia from the beginning there were Tunisian Muslims prepared to question the new developments. The Young Tunisian group, in contact with French intellectuals, felt that they had the right to put their case for a share in the government of their own country. They sent representatives to the Congress of the Colonies held in Marseilles in September 1906. In the following year the Parti Jeune Tunisien was formally organised, and it brought out a French-language

newspaper, *Le Tunisien*, to put forward its views.[16] The
Resident was sensitive to these stirrings and in February
1907 decreed that there should be a Tunisian representative
on the Conférence Consultative which had been set up in
1896 to assist the Resident in financial matters. Unfortunately the offer was marred by the nomination rather than
the election of the Tunisian members.

The French administration was not unduly disturbed by
these requests. The party was a small one and moderate in
its demands for reform. There was no questioning of the
protectorate itself. In the years before the First World War
the economy recovered. Communications were improved
and there was considerable French investment in agriculture, in factories and in mines, particularly the phosphate
enterprises near Gafsa. Economically Tunisia was closely
linked with France and found a satisfactory market for her
exports there. The territory was nevertheless poor and
lacking in raw materials. Resistance seemed to be small, but
there were signs that French tactlessness was building up opposition. In 1911 the Municipality of Tunis tried to take over
the Muslim cemetery of Djellaz and provoked an outburst of
violence.[17] The Tunisian leaders were exiled. An instance
like this linked both the Young Tunisians and the old Muslim
group, known as the 'Old Turbans', who were usually not
hostile to the French, in opposition to the Residency.

The years of the First World War passed peacefully
within Tunisia apart from a few minor skirmishes by the
Italians on the southern Tunisian border. Indeed the
country prospered in the war period. But President Wilson's
theories and the Arab demands for independence at the
Peace Conference did not go unheeded. Tunisia's next-
door neighbours, Tripolitania and Cyrenaica, were granted
a *statuto* by their Italian rulers in 1919, setting up a parliament elected by universal suffrage.[18] French rule was
certain to be questioned again. A book published anony-
mously in Paris in 1920, *La Tunisie martyre. Ses revendications,*

later discovered to be by Sheikh Taalbi, analysed the position of Tunisia under alien rule.

How were these criticisms regarded by the French authorities in Paris and Tunisia? It was clear that they were less tolerant than they had been of the constitutionalists. The Destour party revived and became more vociferous in its demands. In the period from 1920 to 1931 when the half-centenary of the French Protectorate was celebrated, French control tightened. Most of the period was covered by the Residency of a dedicated administrator, Lucien Saint (1920–9). Alarmed at the increase of Italian immigrants, he encouraged the settlement of new groups of Frenchmen, both on the land and in the towns. These Frenchmen demanded as much share in the Government as they had at home and there was a consequent liberalisation of the institutions of the Protectorate.[19] The Conférence Consultative became a Grand Conseil. There was Tunisian representation, again part of it nominated, but this time with elected representatives. A Ministry of Justice (1921), and a Tunisian Chamber of Commerce and Agriculture (1922) were also set up. But these developments did not mean more opportunities for Tunisians. The availability of more Frenchmen for the administrative services tended to leave less room for the Tunisians. In the provinces, particularly, the traditional positions of Sheikh and *qaid* began to carry less weight as the French advisory services grew to meet the expanding economy.

One of the ways in which French supremacy showed itself in these years was in the Resident's attitude to the Bey.[20] The Bey Mohammed en-Nacer was an old man with no great gifts for government. He was tempted in an unwise interview with a Parisian journalist in 1922 to express views which were easily made to appear as a call to his people. In April 1922 he sent a declaration of eighteen points, embodying some of the Destour aims, to the Resident-General. It was the eve of the visit of President Millerand to

Tunisia on his North African tour, and Lucien Saint acted firmly. He visited the Bey accompanied by a contingent of soldiers who surrounded the palace. The interview ended with the triumph of the Resident-General. The incident had repercussions on the Destour Party. A number of their French supporters in the Chambre des Deputés, alarmed at the possibility of violence, withdrew their support from the constitutionalists, thus leaving the floor of the House to the hard-core imperialists. In Tunisia the General Secretariat, the link between the Bey and the Resident, was abolished. When it was restored in 1933 it was shorn of most of its powers.

The celebrations of 1931 were not, as was the widely expressed hope, the harbinger of a long run of peaceful colonial rule. The period of economic prosperity which the Protectorate had been enjoying gave way to a period of depression. The firm rule of Lucien Saint was replaced by the extremes of his successors. Marcel Peyrouton, Resident-General from 1933 to 1936, was harshly repressive; his successor Armand Guillon, weakly liberal. The uncertainties of the situation inevitably aroused the quiescent Destour party. A young lawyer, Habib Bourguiba, took an interest in the movement and in November 1932 he started a newspaper *L'Action Tunisienne* for which he wrote frequently. He and his associates had a more efficient approach than the old Destour group, and they adopted a programme which they discussed in the press. At their National Congress in May 1933 Bourguiba spoke of the new aims of the party which they called the Neo-Destour:

L'indépendance de la Tunisie, complétée par un traité d'amitié et d'union avec la grande République Française garantissant à la France les interêts de toute la colonie étrangère, tel sera l'idéal du mouvement nationaliste tunisien, mouvement destiné surtout à faire de la protection française une entente spontanée entre deux peuples libres, sans aucune idée de prépondérance ou de domination, laquelle n'a plus aucune raison d'être en présence de la solidarité profonde des interêts des deux peuples.[21]

The early moderation of Bourguiba was not matched by the Resident-General, Peyrouton, and growing hostility between the Residency and the nationalists led to the arrest of Bourguiba and the Neo-Destour leaders in 1934. When Bourguiba was released in 1936 he began a more intensive nationalist campaign, which after the fall of the Blum government in 1936 developed into a programme of civil disobedience. Only the outbreak of war prevented his being sentenced.

MOROCCO

Morocco was the last part of the Maghrib to be brought under French control. The area was the scene of several international disputes at the beginning of the twentieth century. The Conference of Algeciras in 1906 gave economic equality to all the European powers in Morocco, but recognised that France and Spain had particular interests there.[22] The country was under the rule of a Sultan who had not pacified the whole of his country. The proportion of Berbers was higher here than in the rest of the Maghrib, and Morocco was traditionally divided into the *bled makhzen*, the subdued area, and the *bled es-siba*, the dissident area where tribal warfare was still in full sway. Moulay Hassan, the last great Sultan before the Protectorate, extended his rule considerably, and his attempts to westernise Morocco led to Great Power involvement there. In April 1911 the reigning Sultan, Moulay Hafid, appealed to the French for help against tribal attack. Germany objected to the action which she held to be against the 1909 agreement she had made with France. Nevertheless after negotiation France acquired a Protectorate over part of Morocco by the Convention of Fez on 30 March 1912. Spain also had part of Morocco and the city of Tangier was made an international zone.

The system of administration set up by the French was

similar to that established in Tunisia, although different problems and different personalities led to a different flavour in the control of Morocco. The first Resident-General was General Lyautey, who had served under Gallieni in Madagascar, and belonged to the old 'Proconsul' style of colonial governor, unashamedly stressing the domination of France, but also its paternalistic responsibilities.[23] 'Oui, un Empire! le mot revient constamment sous votre plume. Empire colonial, n'ayons pas peur des mots', he declared in a speech after his return to France in 1926.[24] His skill as a soldier was vital to a Protectorate where tribal warfare was still rife. By 1914 the French were still not beyond the plains, although they managed to open a communication line to Algeria. After the First World War the struggle went on again; it included a war against Abd el-Krim, the Riff chieftain, in the 1920s. Fighting, in fact, went on in the country until 1934.

The Moroccan Sultan retained more power than his Tunisian counterpart, and Lyautey's courtesy contributed to the smoothness of the relationship between the two men. Indeed, the attitude of the French to the Moroccans was always a special one, and more sympathetic than their attitude to the Arabs elsewhere in the Maghrib. They regarded them with almost Rousseauesque reverence as noble savages. Lyautey himself stressed that French rule was 'la formule du contrôle opposée à la formule d'administration directe'. He was also concerned to retain the languages and customs of both Arabs and Berbers, and wary lest the influence of French culture should spoil the Moroccan heritage.

He had European towns built apart from the Arab *medinas* to preserve the individuality of the latter. He sought to train a Moroccan *élite* who would be able to take over government from the French in the future. The results were not always those he hoped for; the policy tended to create a gulf between the French administrators and the Muslim

Moroccans. Emphasis was put on modernising Moroccan ports, and roads were built. Large French companies were encouraged to invest in the country and to forward 'le miracle Marocain'. The speed with which the transformation was accomplished in the years 1920–5 brought its own problems for the future.

Lyautey's independent actions did not always meet with approval in Paris and in September 1925 the French Government accepted his resignation. Théodore Steeg, a civilian who succeeded him, was pledged to follow a similar policy, but lacking Lyautey's energy and personality he delegated more authority and built up a French administrative service on the Tunisian pattern, considerably increasing the number of French civil servants. Lyautey's policy of the systematic accession of native Moroccans to administrative posts was abandoned.

Nationalism was slow to develop in Morocco and, when it came was closely linked with Islam. Article 1 of the Treaty of Fez had stressed that 'le régime sauvegarde l'exercice de la religion musulmane et des institutions religieuses'. Steeg's successor, Lucien Saint, provoked opposition by issuing a Berber *dahir*, or decree, on 16 May 1930[25] that could be interpreted as dividing Arab from Berber in order to rule both. This decree removed the majority of the Berber tribes from Muslim law and put them under the French criminal code. It also recognised the competence of the tribal *jimaa*, or customary court, and created higher customary courts of appeal. The Muslims regarded this as a French policy of divide and rule. Ahmed Balafrej and Allal al-Fassi, who had formed tentative nationalist groups in 1927, were roused to protest. Demonstrations took place at mosques in Rabat and spread elsewhere in Morocco.

In the thirties opposition to the French régime developed and was strengthened by the support of the young Sultan, Mohammed V, who succeeded to the throne in 1927.[26]

He was not willing to countenance open criticism of the French at first, but his reception at Fez in 1934 warned the French of his powers of leadership. In December 1934 the nationalists put forward a Plan de Réformes Marocaines which they presented simultaneously to the Sultan, the Resident-General and Pierre Laval in Paris. It demanded an increased share for Muslim Moroccans in the administration. No concessions were granted by the French as a result of this petition. Successive Residents, Marcel Peyrouton (1936) and General Noguès (1936–42) increased the pressure of French rule. There was no nationalist response until 1937 when violent demonstrations broke out and the nationalist leaders were imprisoned. Allal al-Fassi was banished to Gabon until 1946.

THE FRENCH ACHIEVEMENT

By 1939 the French had been established for over a century in Algeria, and for over fifty years in both Tunisia and Morocco. New generations of French *colons* had been born who regarded the countries as their own homeland, as indeed they could with justification. French capital had developed the economy of North Africa, and changed the appearance of the towns and the countryside.[27] It is impossible to say at this date if it would have been better to leave the area poor and underdeveloped as it had been before the French arrived. As it was, the change brought in its wake the slum conditions of an industrial revolution, the bidonvilles, or shanty towns, and the creation of two 'nations' which unfortunately in North Africa had the additional overtone of being a division between Arab and Frenchman.

French policy had always concentrated on its *mission civilisatrice*. A frequently quoted French saying was: 'When the Portuguese colonised, they built churches; when the British colonised, they built trading stations; when the

French colonise they build schools.'[28] The result had been the deliberate creation of an Arab *élite*, the *evolués*, who had strong emotional ties with France in the period before the Second World War, and were largely non-Arabic speakers and alienated from their own cultural background. Ferhat Abbas's inability to see any sign of an Algerian nation in the 1930s was a typical response of the Arab intellectual group. It was only when they began to realise that even with a French education they remained second-class citizens that political consciousness developed. France had done enough, however, to retain the loyalty of North Africa through the dark days of 1940, and the organisation of a united and effective nationalist movement was postponed until the war was over.

NOTES TO CHAPTER 4

1. Ch.-A. Julien, *L'Afrique du Nord en marche* (2nd ed. Paris, 1953), p. 84.
2. Dorothy Pickles, *Algeria and France: from Colonialism to Co-operation* (London, 1963), p. 66.
3. For the period of conquest and colonisation see Ch.-A. Julien, *Histoire de L'Algérie contemporaine*, vol. i, *Conquête et colonisation, 1827–1871* (Paris, 1964).
4. A. Nouschi, *La Naissance du Nationalisme algérien* (Paris, 1962), p. 25.
5. A. H. Hourani, *Arabic Thought in the Liberal Age, 1798–1939* (London, 1962), p. 306.
6. Nouschi, op. cit. pp. 28–9.
7. Ibid. p. 55.
8. Julien (1953), p. 111.
9. Nouschi, op. cit. p. 56.
10. Both Nouschi and Julien (1953) discuss the creation and programme of this party.
11. Julien (1953), p. 124.
12. E. F. Gautier, *L'Évolution de l'Algérie de 1830 à 1930* (Algiers, 1931), written for the centenary celebrations, is the classic paean for French rule.

13. Le Tourneau, pp. 329–35.
14. For the debate see J. Ganiage, *Les Origines du Protec-torat français en Tunisie (1861–1881)* (Paris, 1959).
15. Le Tourneau, p. 55.
16. Ibid. p. 58.
17. Ibid.
18. Julien (1953), p. 69.
19. Ibid. pp. 72–3.
20. Le Tourneau, pp. 67–8.
21. H. Bourguiba, *La Tunisie et la France* (Paris, 1954), p. 58.
22. See E. N. Anderson, *The First Moroccan Crisis, 1904–1906* (Hamden, Conn., 1966).
23. See Georges Catroux, *Lyautey le Marocain* (Paris, 1952).
24. H. Lyautey, *Paroles d'action* (Paris, 1938), p. 472.
25. Le Tourneau, pp. 181–5.
26. See Jean Lacouture, *Cinq Hommes et la France* (Paris, 1961), for character study of the sultan.
27. For a concise summary of the North African economy, see Nevill Barbour (ed.), *A Survey of North-West Africa (the Maghrib)*, (2nd ed. London, 1962).
28. David C. Gordon, *North Africa's French Legacy, 1954–1962* (Cambridge, Mass., 1962), p. 7.

5 Resistance Movements and Old Policies

IN spite of the decline of the Ottoman Empire Arab nationalism was slow to develop. Political ideas were being explored in the West, but these were suspect to Islam because they came from an infidel source. French revolutionary ideas, untainted by Christianity, were the first acceptable to the thinkers of the Ottoman Empire.[1] Even then there tended to be an emphasis on Islam among Arab philosophers which was understandable in view of the past achievements of the Arabs which had been carried out in the name of Islam. The writings of the revolutionary religious thinker Jamal al-Din al-Afghani in the late nineteenth century, and his pupil Muhammad Abduh, although they were not nationalists in the accepted sense of the word, put forward a new interpretation of Islam which made later writers feel that it had a relevance for modern thought. Rashid Rida took the ideas a step further and put the emphasis on Arab Islam.

The Turks are a warlike nation, but they are not of greater moment than the Arabs; how can their conquests be compared to those of the Arabs, although their state lasted longer than all the states of the Arabs together? . . . A little knowledge of past and present history shows that most of the countries where Islam was established were conquered by the Arabs who were the active agents of the propagation of Islam.[2]

In 1905 Neguib Azoury published *Le Réveil de la Nation arabe*, which openly advocated the breakaway of the Arab provinces. These ideas were particularly important because they helped the Arabs both to envisage a separate existence from the Turks, and also to think of another unity, that of the speakers of Arabic, and of Islam. In the words of the Emir Feisal whose family hoped to put the ideas into practice, 'We are Arabs before being Muslims and Muhammad is an Arab before being a prophet', and 'We are one people living in the region which is bounded by the sea to the east, the south and the west, and by the Taurus mountains to the north.' The failure of the Hashemite ambitions in Syria after the First World War postponed the creation of a unified Arab state, but the idea remained as a fruitful inspiration during the years of European domination.

Britain was sympathetic to this type of nationalism. It fitted in with the ideas of the Arabs praised by Doughty and Burton in their travel books. But both Britain and France were less happy with the narrower patriotic nationalism of Egypt, Syria and Lebanon. Lebanon had autonomy within the Ottoman Empire from 1860 to 1914. This fact, combined with her contacts with the West and her economic development, gave her more self-awareness as a nation. Egypt could look back on centuries of her history, and in the earlier part of the twentieth century she concentrated on Egyptian nationalism rather than Arab nationalism. General contempt was felt by the Egyptians for the Arab world, and the Arabs felt the same for their 'backward African neighbours', the Egyptians. British experience of the Wafdists in Egypt made her hostile to this brand of nationalism, and both European powers found that they were meeting a similar sort of opposition in the mandated territories.

THE END OF THE FRENCH MANDATE

All these feelings existed before the Second World War broke out, but disunity among the ruled and the prestige which still clung to the rulers prevented any serious challenge to the British and French régime being successful. Events were speeded up by the manifest vulnerability of the masters in the early years of the war.

France was the first of the two powers to be affected by the changing situation in the Middle East. On the outbreak of war the French authorities suspended the Lebanese constitution and took action against various groups in Syria whom they suspected of sympathising with the Germans. The collapse of the home French Government gave cause for much anxiety in the Levant, particularly during the summer of 1940 when Italy joined Germany. Britain was keenly interested in developments in the area, and in July issued a statement of her position:

In order, however, to set at rest doubts which may be felt in any quarter, His Majesty's Government declare that they could not allow Syria or the Lebanon to be occupied by any hostile Power or to be used as a base for attacks upon those countries in the Middle East which they are pledged to defend, or to become the scene of such disorder as to constitute a danger to those countries.[3]

She added that she would take any action she considered necessary to preserve her interests, although this would be without prejudice to the future of the French mandate.

General Dentz, appointed as Vichy High Commissioner at the end of 1940, faced an internal situation of serious unrest.[4] Dr Shahbandar, the Syrian politician, was assassinated and a number of the leaders of the National bloc were implicated in the plot but later cleared. Nationalist demonstrations and strikes broke out as the French hold weakened. General Dentz announced the results of talks he had with the nationalist leaders in April 1941, in which he admitted that the ultimate aim was Syrian independence. He also permitted the setting up of non-party minorities in both Lebanon and Syria to take their share in government. But external events overtook them. Iraq broke out in revolt, and the Allied and Free French forces, to prevent the German use of Syrian air bases, invaded the French mandated territories in June 1941. The advancing armies met with strong opposition from General Dentz, but were finally successful.

The Vichy Frenchmen were treated leniently and allowed to leave the country freely, much to the annoyance of the Free French.

The Vichy wives who were going [wrote Lady Spears] descended on the shops of Beirut like a flock of locusts, and where they had passed the shops were bare, and if you motored from Damascus to Beirut or Baalbek, you found that all over the country the enemy was still comfortably installed in his handsome barracks while our troops, Free French or British or Indian, camped out on bare blazing hillsides, or in mosquito-infested groves.[5]

The British tolerance of the Vichy administrators was explained by their uncertainty about the Free French Government of General de Gaulle, which they still had not recognised. There had already been tension between the General and the British over the role of General Catroux, the Free French liaison officer in the Levant.[6] In June 1941 de Gaulle created him Delegate-General and Pleni-potentiary and briefed him on the attitude of the Free French Government towards the area:

Your mission will consist essentially in restoring the internal and economic situation in the Levant as near to normal as is possible in wartime conditions; to negotiate treaties with suitable representatives of the people, granting inde-pendence and sovereignty to the states of the Levant, and to forge an alliance of these states with France, safe-guarding the rights and interests of France; to ensure the defence of the whole territory against the enemy; to co-operate with the allies in military operations in the Orient.[7]

The work of the Mandate was to continue, but not to be outdone by Vichy, Catroux had to promise that it would be ended as soon as possible:

You will now be sovereign and independent peoples and you can either become separate states or join in one united state. In either case your independence and sovereign states will be guaranteed by a treaty which will define our reciprocal relations. . . . People of Syria and Lebanon, my declaration is proof for you that if the Free French and the British forces cross your frontiers they will not abolish your liberty but safeguard it.[8]

Thus ran his proclamation of intent.

But in practice the Free French met with difficulties. Militarily there was a situation similar to the one which caused hostility between the Allies after the First World War. British troops were in possession, and Syria and Lebanon were also drawn into the economic orbit of the British-controlled territories. In an attempt to define the spheres of the two powers Oliver Lyttelton, British Minister of State in the Middle East, met General de Gaulle in August 1941. An exchange of letters after the meeting presented their conclusions. Britain assured the General: 'We have no desire to encroach in any way upon the position of France. Both Free France and Great Britain are pledged to the independence of Syria and Lebanon. When this essential step has been taken, and without prejudice to it, we freely admit that France should have the predominant position in Syria and Lebanon over any other European Power.[9] This attitude was confirmed by a speech of Churchill's in the House of Commons where he again gave the assurance that Britain had no interest in Syria apart from the general one of security.

But the British sent Major-General Sir Edward Spears at the head of a political mission to the area.[10] His open support of the Arabs and hostility to the French hampered the work of General Catroux, who was negotiating with both the Syrians and the Lebanese to find a way of setting up democratic institutions within the framework of the Mandate. In September 1941 Syria was granted her independence 'under the promise of a treaty' and in

December, Lebanon received a similar assurance. Even the
Free French, though, were reluctant to curtail French
power in the area. The Troupes Spéciales and the arrangement of 'Common Interests', particularly the joint Customs
system, were maintained. Help was given to improve the
economic position of the countries, particularly from the
Middle East Supply Centre in Cairo, an Anglo-American
enterprise set up during the war to distribute aid. Reluc-
tantly in March 1943 the French authorities allowed local
governments to be established in both Syria and Lebanon.
Shukri al-Quwatli became President in Syria, a triumph
for the National bloc. In Lebanon Bishara al-Khury was
unanimously elected President, a victory for the more
moderate nationalist group. From this point the French
could do little to prevent the demand of the constitutionalists for further powers, but they clung tenaciously to their
advisory functions.

At the beginning of 1945 the Troupes Spéciales and the
French garrisons were still there in strength. The moderation of General Beynet could not avert criticism of the
régime fired off by Paris's intransigence over the form of
the promised treaties. On 19 May 1945 strikes were called
in both Syria and Lebanon and on the following day
peaceful opposition turned to violence which was put down
harshly by the French forces. In April, representatives of
both states were invited to the San Francisco Conference,
a welcome recognition of their independent status. In
January 1946 the United Nations debated the problem and
demanded an immediate withdrawal of French and British
troops from the area. The era of French rule was over. In
Syria it meant an increasing Arabisation of the country
and rejection of French education, but in Lebanon the
cultural ties were stronger and remained in evidence after
the abolition of the Mandate. In the wider sphere of
European relations the last years of the French Mandate
caused a deep breach between Britain and France, and

particularly General de Gaulle, which was barely healed by joint action in the Suez venture.[11]

British vulnerability was also revealed clearly by the war. In spite of intensive Axis propaganda the Middle Eastern countries on the whole remained neutral, but it was from reluctance to become involved in a conflict which might impoverish them rather than out of loyalty to the imperialists. Glubb Pasha wrote in a private letter:

The British of course always knew we were going to win the war, but at the time of these operations [German invasions of Greece and Yugoslavia, in 1941] every Arab was perfectly convinced that Britain was finished forever, and that it could only be a question of weeks before Germany took over Arabia. The Iraqis were perfectly sure of this or they would not have declared war on us. . . . I do not think you have fully realised to what extent during the six weeks before Baghdad fell, the whole Arab world seemed to be solidly against us.[12]

The Middle East and North Africa played a considerable part in the campaigns of the war.[13] Persia had to be protected by 'Paiforce' to support supply routes to Russia and to ensure oil supplies. North Africa was the scene of the campaigns against Rommel. Egypt, which refused to declare war on Germany although it broke off diplomatic relations with the Axis, remained quiescent under British rule, and was valuable as a supply centre. In 1941 the German advance in Eastern Europe, which looked as though it might end in Russian defeat and the diversion of German attention to the Middle East front, led to high-handed British action in Egypt. The Egyptian Government was pro-German in its sympathies and in January 1942 Lord Killearn, the British Ambassador, asked King Farouk to remove the existing ministry and to appoint

Nahas Pasha as Prime Minister. Nahas Pasha was the current leader of the Wafd Party and pro-British, in so far as he realised the importance of an Allied victory for his country. The British request was accompanied by threats of the possible deposition of the King himself.

This action produced the right response at the time from the British point of view, but its high-handedness was not likely to be forgotten by the Egyptian nationalists. The British were to find that it was no longer possible to guide Egypt by persuading a malleable politician or bullying a dissolute king. 'Street opinion' now had to be taken into consideration. An extreme group, the Muslim Brotherhood, founded by Hasan al-Banna in 1928, attracted increasing numbers of young malcontents in the 1940s and preached violently against imperialism. The Egyptian Government itself was moving towards a championship of Arab nationalism. From the time of the 1936 Treaty, Egypt began to be accepted more favourably by her Arab neighbours, with the result that when the Arab Unity Conference was called in October 1944 it was held in Alexandria with Nahas Pasha as its president. The Arab League which resulted from this treaty had its headquarters in Cairo, and an Egyptian Secretary-General, Abdel Rahman Azzam.[14] The original member states were Egypt, Iraq, Syria, Lebanon, Saudi Arabia, Transjordan and Yemen. Anthony Eden gave encouragement to Arab unity in his Mansion House speech of 1941, but it was less easy for the British to live with the day-to-day irritation of Egyptian nationalism.

At the end of the war the Egyptian Government, now under a more militant leader Mahmoud Nokrashy, brought up the question of treaty revision. They hoped that their contribution during the war entitled them to a hearing, but the immediate response of Britain, preoccupied with the new threats of Russian ambition, was to stress 'the essential soundness of the fundamental principles' of the 1936 Treaty. In February 1945 the Fuad University at Cairo was reopened and the occasion gave an opportunity for violent demonstrations against the British occupation. The negotiations between the two powers in the post-war period had no common basis, for the Egyptians could accept nothing less than the complete evacuation of their country, while Britain on her part was equally sure that she could not allow a 'vacuum' in Egypt which might be filled by a rival.* Salah al-Din Bey, the Egyptian Foreign Minister, summed up the differences in approach in 1950: 'Your foreign policy is of such a wide range that it almost embraces all international problems, but our foreign policy is a very limited one, and can almost be resolved in the two questions now under discussion, the question of evacuation and that of the unity of Egypt and the Sudan under the Egyptian crown.'[15]

Middle Eastern hopes were raised when Ernest Bevin became Foreign Secretary in the new British Labour Government in 1945.[16] A man of strong individuality and preferences, it was thought that he might break through to new criteria of foreign policy based on his socialist beliefs, but he soon became enmeshed in all the old disputes of the area. Loathed by the Jews for his Palestine decisions, he was equally mistrusted by the Arabs. Elizabeth Monroe has pointed out that his policy only seemed pro-Arab to non-Arabs.[17] The pattern of violent disorder in Egypt and appeals for new talks continued. Sidky Pasha, now Egyptian Prime Minister, approached Bevin and on 7 May 1946 the British Government made a new offer; 'the withdrawal of all British forces from Egyptian territory, and to settle by negotiation the stages and date of completion of this withdrawal, and the arrangements to be made by the Egyptian Government to make possible mutual assistance in time of war or imminent threat of war in accordance with the alliance.'[18] Egyptian nationalists were not prepared to accept even this saving clause and the negotiations

* See Chapter 7 for the role of the Middle East in international affairs after the Second World War.

continued. Progress was made on the question of evacuation, and the Sidky–Bevin Protocol provided for withdrawal of British troops by 1949. But the question of the Sudan remained a stumbling block. Britain had encouraged Sudanese self-rule and set up an Advisory Council for the Northern Sudan in 1944. Neither she nor the Sudanese were anxious to see a revival of the Egyptian claim to sovereignty over the area. The most Bevin felt he could concede was 'the existence of a symbolic dynastic union between Egypt and the Sudan, provided always that no change was introduced into the existing system of administration . . . and no change took place in the arrangements under which the defence of the Sudan is assured.'[19]

Sidky Pasha was replaced by Nokrashy Pasha once again and Egypt decided to put the whole matter before the Security Council. The Egyptian case was rejected by one vote. But difficulties in Palestine encouraged Britain to make a last attempt to negotiate with Egypt which, humiliated by the defeat in the Arab–Israeli war,* was also prepared to try again. In January 1950 the Wafd Party returned to power with a landslide victory which gave hope that agreement with Britain might be reached, but the fundamental differences of approach remained and in April 1950 the British Ambassador presented his last proposals. He began with the proviso that Britain could not 'accept the responsibility of making any arrangements which prejudice their ability to contribute to a successful defence of this region against an aggressor. Such a defence will only be possible if in the future the Egypt base continues to function in such a manner as to be immediately available in war and if the air defence of Egypt is assured.'[20] British troops would be withdrawn by 1956 and the British Government would be prepared to discuss the question of Sudan 'at the earliest practicable opportunity'. The offer was rejected completely by the Egyptians. Britain now added to her

* See below, pp. 89–91.

arguments the new point of her international obligations. 'The problem of the presence of British troops in Egypt is not now a purely Anglo-Egyptian problem', said Herbert Morrison in a Commons debate. 'We are a Power bearing responsiblities in the Middle East on behalf of the rest of the Commonwealth and the Western Allies as a whole.' In return the Egyptian Government made a unilateral rejection of the 1936 Treaty. The newly returned Conservative Government in Britain declared that it was impossible for the Egyptians to do this. A complete impasse had been reached.

THE END OF THE PALESTINE MANDATE

The problems of Palestine, already overwhelming, were increased by the persecution of the Jews carried out in Hitler's Germany and the occupied countries of Europe. World Jewry, and in particular the Americans, began to plan for the development of Palestine after the war was over. On 11 May 1942 a conference at the Biltmore Hotel in New York drew up a resolution of its intentions.[21] The moderate leadership of Chaim Weizmann was challenged by the new star of the militant David Ben Gurion.[22] Less of an intellectual than the older man, he had left Russia in 1906 for Palestine where he worked his way as labourer, journalist and politician. He was a founder member of the Histadrut Trade Union movement and of the workers' party. His proposals condemned British rule and demanded Palestine for the Jews.

The Conference acclaimed him, and it completely rejected the 1939 White Paper and its limitations on immigration into Palestine, calling it 'cruel and indefensible'. The Conference urged 'that the gates of Palestine be opened; that the Jewish Agency be vested with control of immigration into Palestine and with the necessary authority for upbuilding the country, including the development of its unoccupied and uncultivated lands; and that Palestine be established as a Jewish Commonwealth integrated in the structure of the new democratic world.'

When peace was proclaimed in Europe the Jewish Agency sent a demand to London asking Britain to carry out the programme, and to send an immediate loan for the settlement of the first million Jews in Palestine. Churchill temporised and said any decision must await a Great Power conference, but the victory of the British Labour Party in the 1945 elections raised Jewish hopes, for its members had been wholly opposed to the 1939 White Paper in debate in the House of Commons. The easy criticisms of a party in opposition, however, had to be modified by a government in power. It felt that its hand was being forced by Jewish pressure and by the growing threats of violence in Palestine itself. The underground resistance movements and, in particular, the extremist Stern Group were building up opposition to the British. In November 1944 two young men of the group murdered Lord Moyne, British Minister in Cairo. The Jewish Agency expressed its horror at the event, but counsels could do nothing to stop the increase of violence which culminated in the blowing up in July 1946 of the King David Hotel which housed the British administration in Jerusalem.[23] Gradually, too, the more moderate Haganah, the defence army organisation which had at first attempted to co-operate with the British, became convinced that nothing short of open attack would persuade the British of Jewish purpose.

Britain was anxious for American support in the settlement of the Palestine problem. In November 1945 the United States Government agreed to work with Britain in a joint committee. Its recommendations, published in the following April, attempted to be fair, but did not provide a practical solution to the difficulties.[24] They declared 'that Jew shall not dominate Arab and Arab shall not dominate Jew in Palestine. That Palestine shall be neither a Jewish state nor an Arab state.' The spread of violence was noted with dismay and seemed to preclude any idea of an independent Palestine. They therefore recommended 'until this hostility disappears, the Government of Palestine be continued as at present under mandate, pending the execution of a trusteeship agreement under the United Nations.' The immigration quota was laid down at the 1939 figure which had already nearly been reached.

Ernest Bevin's outspoken criticism of Jewish pressure made him many enemies, and the practical response of the Jewish Agency in Palestine to their disappointment was to encourage the increase of illegal immigration. The Palestine administration tightened up regulations against terrorist attacks, but the slowness of announcing any policy as an outcome of the Anglo-American report led to the King David Hotel incident. The General Officer Commanding in Palestine issued instructions to his troops which blamed the Jews for the outrages in insulting terms.[25] The paper was seen by the Zionists and caused further hostility between the two sides. Meanwhile more Anglo-American talks were taking place in London and produced the Grady–Morrison plan. The suggestions, published on 30 July 1946, put forward a 'provincial autonomy' scheme which would set up two provinces with limited control of their affairs. 'It was a reduced version of the Peel recommendations put forward ten years after Peel could have been effective.'[26] Discussions went on in London, but neither Jew nor Arab was prepared to accept solutions on this basis.

In April 1947 Britain put the Palestine suggestions before the United Nations Assembly with the request that she 'should not have the sole responsibility for enforcing a solution which is not accepted by both parties and which we cannot reconcile with our conscience.'[27] A special committee, the United Nations Special Commission on Palestine (UNSCOP) was set up to investigate the matter. Its members visited Palestine and attempted to get opinions from all sides although they were not well received. Their recommendation, the result of compromise, eventually appeared as one of partition into a Jewish and an Arab State. On 29 November 1947 the resolution was adopted by the General Assembly.[28] The British Mandate was to end 'as soon as possible but in any case not later than August 1948', and troops were to be withdrawn gradually. Provisions were made for the establishment of representative institutions in each state and for the protection of religious minorities.

The British Government having referred the matter to the United Nations was not altogether happy in renouncing Palestine to international discussion. The vacillations and doubts can be followed in Jon and David Kimche's *Both Sides of the Hill*.[29] Mr Creech Jones, the Colonial Secretary, announced British withdrawal from Palestine before the United Nations vote, believing that it would be impossible for the General Assembly to come to any unanimous conclusion. Meanwhile in Palestine itself terrorism continued to grow, and British troops, demoralised by this type of warfare, allowed the Arabs to get away with many acts of reprisal against the Jewish community. Finally in December 1947 the British Government announced that it would end the Mandate on 15 May 1948.

THE ARAB–ISRAELI WAR

This precipitous decision was largely the result of considerations which lay outside the Middle East. The economic position of Britain in 1947 was extremely serious and encouraged the reduction of expenditure wherever possible. Desire for Marshall Aid from the United States was also an important factor in persuading the British Government to follow a policy that the Americans would approve. The example of the withdrawal from India was cited by some members of the Cabinet as one which could be sensibly

followed in Palestine, but it was a long time before a
decision was made. Communication between Jerusalem and
London was confused. Questions referred to London were
shelved until the changing situation made a political
decision unnecessary.[30] There was no clear picture of what
would happen if the British left suddenly. The Colonial
Secretary, Creech Jones, thought that there would be no
war; Bevin was less optimistic, but thought that if it did
come to a contest of arms the Arabs would win.

In this uncertain atmosphere both the Arabs and the
Jews began to arm. The members of the Arab League held
a number of meetings to try to produce a common policy.
King Abdullah of Jordan, granted his crown by the
British in return for the renunciation of a scheme to link
Syria, Palestine and Jordan in a Greater Syria, now had
ambitions to acquire Palestine for a Greater Jordan. His
Arab Legion commanded by General Glubb was considered
to be the best army in the area. The other Arab states were
not enthusiastic about this plan, nor was the Mufti of
Jerusalem. Egypt and Lebanon opposed open warfare, pre-
ferring the less direct way of sending arms to support local
guerrilla troops and organisations such as the Muslim
Brotherhood. Ben Gurion had fewer political problems,
although there was not complete unanimity on a course of
action. His chief anxiety was for the training and supply
of a military force. There was the Haganah with its well
trained commando unit, the Palmach, but otherwise there
was little experience.*

Fighting broke out before the British evacuation was
begun. Jewish successes in Haifa resulted in an Arab
exodus from the town, an unhappy portent of things to
come. As the British withdrew the Jews took over their

---

* The Jewish side of the war is better documented than the Arab
side. The Kimches in *Both Sides of the Hill*, and Michel Bar-Zohar in
Ben Gourion, prophète armé use Jewish sources. Glubb Pasha in *A Soldier
among the Arabs* (London, 1957), discusses the Arab Legion. The Arab
version of the war has been heavily overladen with propaganda.

strongholds and military posts. The fighting in the first part of the war over Jerusalem left the city divided in Arab and Jewish hands. The United Nations debated the issue, but its early discussions were balked by Britain, who appeared to want interference which would damage the Arab position.[31] A truce was eventually arranged on 14 May 1948 and Count Folke Bernadotte was appointed as United Nations Mediator.[32] His first proposals, which gave the Arabs the Negev and Jerusalem in return for handing Galilee to the Jews, were not welcomed by the latter, and war broke out again. On 17 September Bernadotte was murdered by the Stern Group and the Israelis showed great tardiness in pursuing his murderers.

The Israelis took the offensive in October 1948, and because of the hesitations of the Security Council, were able to push forward into the Negev at the turn of the year. The last part of the war was virtually a duel between Israel and Egypt. When the cease-fire was signed between them in February 1949 the Israeli operation 'Fait accompli' was uncompleted and Egypt kept the Gaza Strip. Ben Gurion has been criticised for not pressing home his military advantage by taking the east bank of the Suez Canal, but he did not want to lose the political bargaining power of the new Israel by appearing too intransigent.[33]

Ben Gurion had announced the new State of Israel in May 1948 and it had been recognised by the United States and the European powers. A year later Israel was admitted to the United Nations. The Arabs, forced to accept a cease-fire, would not, and still do not, recognise the Jewish State. The United Nations supported Arab refugee camps in the Gaza Strip which were a perpetual reminder of their humiliation. Jerusalem was left a divided city, and on the Israeli-Syrian border a demilitarised zone provided an area of tension. Britain's muddled actions and apparently partisan behaviour in the United Nations debate had lost her the respect of both Arab and Jew. But whatever the result her motives were not as diabolic as her enemies supposed.

Critics of the British Government sometimes alleged that it deliberately organised the chaos it created because it wanted a fight, and wanted an Arab victory. But anyone who thought so had lost all sense of the place of Palestine in the British scale of values of 1948. An Arab win would have saddled Great Britain with at least two unthinkable consequences – accountability to the world for a new Jewish dispersion, and alienation of the United States at a moment when American goodwill was a matter of life and death to Great Britain not only financially, but in Germany.[34]

Nor did Britain want to stay in Palestine, as Bevin stressed in March 1948: 'We have to get in a position to enable us to get out of Palestine. This is the fundamental point of British policy.'[35] The difficulty in the Middle East was that nobody could quite believe that the British Government meant what it said.

NOTES TO CHAPTER 5

1. See A. H. Hourani, *Arabic Thought in the Liberal Age* (London, 1962), for the best study of the development of ideas.
2. Sylvia Haim (ed.), *Arab Nationalism: An Anthology* (Berkeley and Los Angeles, 1964), pp. 22–3.
3. A. H. Hourani, *Syria and Lebanon: A Political Essay* (London, 1946), p. 232.
4. For a very detailed account of the Vichy administration of the Levant, see Isaac Lipschits, *La Politique de la France au Levant, 1939–1941* (Paris, 1963).
5. Mary Borden (Lady Spears), *Journey Down a Blind Alley* (London, 1947), p. 145.
6. General Catroux's own account of his mission, *Dans la bataille de Méditerranée. Egypte–Levant–Afrique du Nord, 1940–1944, Témoignages et commentaires* (Paris, 1949).
7. Trans. from document in Hourani, *Syria and Lebanon*, pp. 372–3.

8. Trans. from document in Hourani, *Syria and Lebanon*, pp. 371–2.
9. Hurewitz, ii, p. 232.
10. Jon Kimche, *Seven Fallen Pillars* (2nd ed. London, 1953), p. 103.
11. General de Gaulle, *Mémoires de guerre* (see bibliography), makes plain his complaints.
12. Kimche, op. cit. p. 35.
13. See George Kirk, *The Middle East in the War, 1939–1946* (London, 1952) for detailed discussion of problems.
14. Muhammad Khalil, *The Arab States and the Arab League* (2 vols., Beirut, 1962).
15. Quoted in Elizabeth Monroe, 'Mr Bevin's Arab Policy', in *St Antony's Papers*, Middle Eastern Affairs, 2, (London, 1961), p. 47.
16. Alan Bullock's definitive biography, *The Life and Times of Ernest Bevin* (2 vols., London, 1960 and 1966), has not yet reached this period of its subject's career.
17. Monroe, op. cit. p. 46.
18. R.I.I.A., *Great Britain and Egypt* (London, 1952), p. 88.
19. R.I.I.A., op. cit. p. 93.
20. R.I.I.A., op. cit. p. 136.
21. Hurewitz, ii, pp. 234–5.
22. Michel Bar-Zohar, *Ben Gourion, prophète armé* (Paris, 1966), had access to his papers.
23. See M. Begin, *The Revolt* (London, 1951) for Stern Group justification of its violence.
24. Hurewitz, ii, pp. 264–6.
25. Kimche, op. cit. p. 41.
26. C. Sykes, *Crossroads to Israel* (London, 1965), pp. 359–360.
27. G. Kirk, *The Middle East, 1945–1950* (London, 1954), p. 239.
28. Hurewitz, ii, pp. 281–95.
29. Jon and David Kimche, *Both Sides of the Hill* (London, 1960).
30. Jon and David Kimche, op. cit. pp. 35–6.
31. G. Kirk, op. cit. pp. 273–5.
32. Bernadotte wrote his own account of the mission *To Jerusalem* (London, 1951).
33. Kimche, op. cit. p. 263.
34. Monroe, p. 169.
35. House of Commons speech, quoted in Monroe, p. 169.

6 North Africa *en marche*

'LA FRANCE ignorait dans ces pays qu'elle était mortelle', wrote Jacques Berque of the inter-war period in the Maghrib. The shock of the fall of France in 1940 was to bring the fact home to North African nationalists, even if the French themselves found it a harder lesson to assimilate. In North Africa, as elsewhere in the Arab world, there had been a confusion of aims and ideals. There was no Maghribi nationalist movement, only isolated groups of people protesting against French rule. In 1927 the Moroccan nationalist Allal al-Fassi organised an Association des Etudiants musulmans d'Afrique du Nord in Paris, which for a few years held annual congresses.[1] Later its members became absorbed in their own growing national parties. The visit of Sheikh Arslan, the Lebanese apostle of Islamic reform, to the North African countries in 1930 raised the hope of the Muslim nationalists who saw the road to independence through unity with the international Islamic movement.[2] Although it became clear in the post-war period that the nationalist parties were taking most of their political arguments from the West, Islam remained an important factor. The response to the Algerian colonial cry of 'Algérie française' was 'Algérie musulmane', not 'Algérie arabe'. The achievement of the national leaders in the fifties was to unite and organise opposition to the French, although most of the early nationalists wanted to belong to the French Union and it was done as an individual national effort, not in a pan-Maghrib movement.

MOROCCO

Morocco, the last North African possession to be acquired by France, was the first to gain its independence. Mohammed V declared his allegiance to France when war broke out and General Noguès remained at his post as Resident-General. The American landings in November 1942 were the sign for renewed national protest against the French régime, and particularly they encouraged the Sultan to stand up to the Resident-General and assert his authority. When Roosevelt, Churchill and de Gaulle met for the Casablanca Conference in 1943 the Sultan acted as host for his country. After a private meeting with Roosevelt without any French advisers present, the Sultan reported that he had American support for his country's future independence.[3]

Here was the beginning of a steady decline in the French hold over Morocco. General Noguès was replaced by a career diplomat, Gabriel Puaux, whose lack of sympathy with his new assignment strained Franco-Moroccan relations. Ahmed Balafrej galvanised the nationalists and in 1942 he began to organise a new party, the Istiqlal or Independence Party. He sent its manifesto both to the Sultan and the Resident-General in January 1943. The party's aim was 'de demander l'indépendance du Maroc dans son integrité territoriale sous l'égide de sa Majesté Sidi Mohammed Ben Youssef' and 'to request his Majesty to assume the leadership of the reform movement which is so necessary for the good of the country, and to entrust to his Majesty the task of establishing a democratic régime similar to that adopted in the Muslim countries of the Orient, guaranteeing the rights of all groups and classes in Moroccan society, and defining the duties of each individual.'[4] The Resident-General immediately said that no unilateral action against the Protectorate could be admitted, but M. Massigli of the French Foreign Ministry, on a visit to Morocco, assured the Sultan that reforms would be carried out.

Two weeks later Balafrej was arrested and violence broke out in Rabat and Fez. The Resident-General put down the disturbances firmly. On 16 February he appointed four commissioners to consider reform, and in the following month a *dahir* created a commission to codify Moroccan penal law.[5] The appointment of a new Resident-General, Eirik Labonne, a diplomat, in March 1946 introduced a more liberal element into the Residency. He allowed the return of Allal al-Fassi from Gabon, and initiated a programme to restore the Moroccan economy badly damaged by the war. But the nationalists were not satisfied. A group visited Paris in the spring of 1947 to ask for independence. In April 1947 the Sultan made a speech in Tangier stressing the unity of Morocco. 'It goes without saying that Morocco is an Arab country, closely linked to the Arab Orient. It is natural to strengthen and reaffirm these ties, particularly as the Arab League has become an organisation with an important role in world politics.'[6] France's response to this open defiance was to replace Labonne with a soldier, General Juin.

He insisted on a firm application of the 1912 Treaty, but in June he moderated his sternness and issued two *dahirs* to reorganise the Makhzen, or central Moroccan government. The Grand Vizier was given a small council to act as liaison between the Resident and the Sultan. The Council of Government was also enlarged by Muslim Moroccan members. In return the Resident-General hoped to obtain promises from the Sultan that he would not engage in politics. In January 1951 Juin demanded that the Sultan should either renounce the Istiqlal Party or his throne.[7] The Sultan gave in on this occasion, but he went on giving tacit support to the nationalists. The independent Arab states tried to bring the Moroccan question before the United Nations and sympathy was provoked even in

France, where the Sultan excited more enthusiasm than any other North African nationalist ever managed to arouse. The repressive measures of consecutive Residents-General developed in the course of 1952 and 1953 into a policy of dividing the country in such a way as to create hostility towards the Sultan. Support was given to the Glaoui family of the Berber highlands and to Abd al-Hai al Kittani, the leader of a religious brotherhood. These two incited the tribes to march north to demand the deposition of the Sultan.

On 10 August 1953 the Resident-General sent Mohammed V into exile and put a puppet ruler in his place. This rash French use of anarchy turned against them like a boom-erang. Violence grew in the next two years and several attempts were made on the life of the new Sultan. By 1955 terrorism was rife, revolts occurred on the anniversary of Mohammed's deposition, and in November a Moroccan 'Army of Liberation' began systematic raids on French posts in the Rif and the Middle Atlas. A succession of Residents-General tried to restore order, but at last the French Foreign Minister, Antoine Pinay, was forced to agree to the return of the exiled Mohammed. The Celle–St-Cloud communiqué signed between them on 6 November 1953 said:

His Majesty the Sultan of Morocco has confirmed his desire to form a Moroccan administrative government with power to negotiate, representing all the different shades of Moroccan opinion. The government will have the task of carrying out institutional reforms, which will make Morocco a democratic state with a constitutional monarchy, and also of conducting negotiations with France designed to strengthen the mutual ties between the two countries, which have been freely agreed to and defined.'[8]

On 2 March 1956 the French protectorate in Morocco came to an end.

TUNISIA

Tunisia's closeness to Libya and to the Italian mainland made her an important factor in the Second World War. After France's armistice with Germany in 1940 the Vichy régime sent out Admiral Esteva to represent it as Resident-General. The nationalist Tunisians' attitude to the warring powers was ambivalent. They were not concerned with Europe's quarrel but hoped to further their own political aims, a slant which later caused both the Bey and the Neo-Destour, Bourguiba's new constitutional party, to be labelled as Axis sympathisers. The weakness of the Vichy Government provided a good opportunity for action. The initiative passed to the ruling Bey, Moncef, who put forward a programme of reform in August 1942.[9] He demanded a complete 'tunisification' of the administration, instruction in Arabic in the schools, and the nationalisation of the main services. He also made a personal appeal to the *qaids* to accept orders from him over the heads of the French administration.

In October 1942 there was an open breach between the Bey and the Resident-General, and the Bey sent a telegram to Marshal Pétain in Paris demanding Esteva's recall. The Resident was still strong enough to weather this storm, but he had to make concessions. On 30 December 1942 a new Tunisian ministry, containing among others the Neo-Destourian Dr Materi, was created by the Bey, the first time since the beginning of the French protectorate that such appointments had been made without French approval. But a later Resident managed to force the Bey to abdicate and he spent the last years of his life imprisoned in France. His successor and the new ministry were completely under French control.

Meanwhile the North African campaigns had swept over Tunisia leaving the country exhausted. The initial promises of the Allies were clouded by the prospect of renewed

French dominance. Events in the Middle East, the protest of the Palestinians, and the independence of Syria and Lebanon increased Tunisian determination to achieve self-government and gradually built up the resolve of the Neo-Destour party. The French also reorganised themselves. General Mast, the Resident-General after the Allied victory, carried out a programme of public works to repair the damage done during the war.[10] He also initiated some political changes in February 1945. A new post of Minister of Social Affairs was created, to be held by a Tunisian, and the Tunisian share of votes in the electoral college for the Grand Conseil was made equal to that of the French. In the eyes of the nationalists this was little enough, and certainly did not justify Georges Bidault's enthusiastic remark that the new electoral reform 'sera tel qu'il n'y aura pas un autre pays de civilisation comparable sur les bords de la Mediterranée qui ne puisse tourner vers la Tunisie avec envie'.[11]

There were public demonstrations against the administration which led to the replacement of General Mast by Jean Mons as Resident-General on 16 January 1947. He had been a colleague of Léon Blum and much was hoped for from his term of office. The measures of July and August 1947 increased the number of Tunisian ministers on the Council from four to six, but it still left the French in the majority.[12] The step was too little and too late. The Resident's moderation irritated the nationalists and violent demonstrations were organised. In Sfax rioting strikers clashed with the authorities and twenty-nine were killed and fifty-seven wounded. The example of Palestine was in the minds of the Tunisians. The following year the death of Moncef Bey in Pau gave his successor Lamine the legitimate title he sought. Yet the change seemed the end of the era of reform, for the Residency, freed from worries over the Bey's title, took a firmer line.

To this situation Habib Bourguiba returned in September

1949, with the permission of the Resident.[11] His period of exile had given him time to think seriously about the future of the Neo-Destour. He realised the importance of a good political organisation which would reach the whole of Tunisia, not just the middle-class elements of the population in the capital. The political enthusiasm of the workers showed that they should be brought into the movement. A visit to Cairo in 1947 had, however, convinced him that his line must be a different one from the eastern Arab nationalists; he did not envisage a complete break with France. 'Ce que la Tunisie réclame, c'est un statut d'État souverain, lié à la France par un traité d'alliance librement négocié qui garantisse à cette dernière ses intérêts stratégiques, économiques et culturels. Une assemblée constituante élue dotera le pays d'une constitution démocratique moderne.'[14]

Bourguiba's return led to 'la crise franco-tunisienne' of the years 1950–5. Jean Mons was replaced by Louis Périllier as Resident-General in May 1950. Before Périllier left for Tunisia he was guest at a banquet in Thionville where the Minister of Foreign Affairs, Robert Schumann, spoke of the future for the Protectorate:

M. Périllier dans ses nouvelles fonctions aura pour mission de comprendre et de conduire la Tunisie vers le plein épanouissement de ses richesses et de l'amener vers l'indépendance qui est l'objectif final pour tous les territoires au sein de l'Union française. Il faut cependent accepter les délais nécessaires et, si cette entreprise réuississait, la France au cours de son histoire si longue aura accompli une nouvelle fois sa mission civilisatrice.[15]

The Protocol of August 1950 created a new Tunisian ministry under the presidency of Mhammed Chenik. Their task was to 'négocier modifications institutionelles, qui par étages successives, doivent conduire la Tunisie vers l'autonomie interne.'[16]

After a delay during which a strike of agricultural

workers led to more violence, the Beylical Decrees of February 1951 were issued. The powers of the Tunisian Government were increased though French control remained, and priority was given to Tunisians in civil service recruitment. The difficulties of the Resident were illustrated by the reactions of the Rassemblement Français de Tunisie.[17]

The nationalists might complain of the slowness of even the most moderate Resident to act, but his position was a difficult one. Torn between the Tunisians on one hand, and the *colons* on the other, he had to move gingerly. Périllier's administration brought a violent protest from the Rassemblement Français de Tunisie, the *colon* body. In May 1950 a delegation from the *colonie française* wrote to Robert Schumann putting their case and protesting about the weakness of the Resident which, they said, had lost the Protectorate all support in the country. The Beylical Decrees roused the group to further anger, their opinions carried great weight in Paris and Périllier slowed the pace of political change, saying that it was 'temps d'accorder une pause à la politique' and time to give precedence 'aux problèmes humains de reconstruction économique et sociale'.[18] He did, however, suggest the reform of municipal government in July 1951, and recognised the Neo-Destour Party a month later. This led to further representation to Paris by the *colons*, who denied the Resident's right to speak for the colony. Robert Schumann replied, on 15 December 1951, that he could not deny a share in government to the Tunisians. 'Le Gouvernement français est fortement attaché à ce principe qui lui parait seul susceptible d'assurer par une association féconde franco-tunisienne le développement harmonieux de ces institutions.'[19]

Battle was joined. Jean de Hautecloque, who replaced Périllier in January 1952, was a man of more rigid views. He demanded the resignation of Mhammed Chenik and the recall of two ministers who had gone to make representations in Paris; there was unrest throughout the country.[20] Plans for further reforms were discussed in the National Assembly in Paris, but although they met with moderate enthusiasm there was no practical result. Once more the Bey took the initiative in Tunis and summoned a group of all sections of Tunisian opinion, the *quarante*, to discuss the future of the country, and to draw up a criticism of the Paris reforms, which they rejected. Hautecloque was replaced by Pierre Voizard in a final attempt to pacify the nationalists by the promise of progressive reforms, but the Neo-Destour rejected all compromises. Violence was now widespread. The Tunisians formed guerrilla bands called *fellagha*, or bandits, by the French, and the *colons* retaliated with counter-terrorist activities.

The French Prime Minister, Mendès-France, decided to end the struggle. Speaking in Carthage on 31 July 1954 he agreed to Tunisian self-government. 'L'autonomie interne de l'État tunisien est reconnue et proclamée sans arrière-pensée par le Gouvernement français qui entend tout à la fois l'affirmer dans son principe et lui permettre dans l'action la consécration du succès.'[21] A Neo-Destour government was set up and a few months later Bourguiba was released from his French prison. The example of Morocco encouraged the Tunisians to ask for complete independence in the following spring. Bourguiba, true to his earlier promises, did not make a complete break with France. An agreement with the French Government in March 1957 provided Tunisia with technicians, teachers and administrators.

ALGERIA

The Vichy régime appointed a Governor-General for Algeria, as it had appointed Residents elsewhere in North Africa. As elsewhere, the nationalists were stirred to protest. Their leader Ferhat Abbas made representation to Pétain and later to the Free French Government which was set up in Algiers. He also had a glimpse of a larger audience when he met Robert Murphy, President Roosevelt's special representative, and discussed his hopes with him.[22] At the end of 1943 he drew up *L'Algérie devant le conflit mondial. Manifeste du Peuple Algérien.*[22] It analysed the colonial situation and put the aims suggested. 'Le caractère saillant et continu de la colonisation française est la subordination de tout le pays avec son humanité, ses richesses, son outillage, son administration, à cet élément français et européen.' France's response was not immediate. The Governor-General, General Giraud, was preoccupied with the wider issues of the war, but General de Gaulle's government was sympathetic towards a slow and steady improvement of the Muslim Algerians' position. The Ordinance of 7 March 1944, when it finally came, offered very much the same terms as the 1936 Blum–Violette scheme had done. It spoke of the Muslim *élite* sharing political rights with the French.

Ferhat Abbas and the supporters of the Manifesto were disillusioned by the repetition of old formulas. There was discontent outside Algiers too. In May 1945, while the Allied victory was being celebrated, violence broke out in Sétif and spread to the neighbouring countryside.[24] Ninety-seven Frenchmen were killed and a large number of Muslims; the official figure of 1500 was contested by the nationalists who put it as high as 50,000. A comparison of the figures even at the lower estimate showed the strength of the Administration and the harshness of its methods. Blame for the incident was laid at the door of the Manifestoists, but it belonged more properly to the Parti Populaire Algérien (PPA), a group founded by Messali Hadj in 1936 as a successor to his workers' party, the Étoile Nord-africaine.[25] His group was more militant than Ferhat Abbas's supporters and later formed a special branch, the Organisation Secrète (OS) under Ahmed Ben Bella, whose specific aim was violent action. The dissarray of the nationalist movement for some years made their protest less effective than their numbers would suggest. Close contact with France, and the constant traffic of workers to and fro, meant that the politically conscious often joined one of the many parties in metropolitan France. In Algeria itself the PPA and Ferhat Abbas's group organised into a party after the Ordinance, as the Amis du Manifeste de la Liberté (AML). Ferhat Abbas's party became Union démocratique des Amis du Manifesto (UDMA). In 1946 these were the two most prominent elements, but there were minority organisations for the communists, for the Muslims and for other expressions of opinion.

The French administration was not wholly complacent about the Sétif incident. Yves Chataigneau, the Resident appointed by de Gaulle, worked for the creation of a constituent assembly and also for the improvement of social and economic conditions. A department of reform had been set up in August 1945 and two years later it became a body charged with executing a specific Plan. A beginning was made with the modernisation of agriculture and the Muslims were given a greater share in municipal government.

The French National Assembly passed an organic law on 20 September 1947, usually called 'Le Statut de l'Algérie'.[26] The act created a Constituent Assembly of 120 members elected by two electoral colleges, the first containing the group, both French and Muslim, enfranchised by the 1944 Ordinaire, the second by Muslim men above the age of twenty-one. Muslims became French citizens without renouncing their legal Muslim status. The Assembly had powers of financial control, although it could not refuse to grant a budget, and it had some say in administration. The Statute emphasised once again that Algeria was part of France and it established a new Algerian ministry in Paris. The Statute, scorned by the nationalists because it was not of their own devising, did represent an advance in

French thinking. At least in theory it constituted an advance; in practice it was not fully carried out, for in 1948 the elections were rigged.

The seven years between the enacting of the Statute and the outbreak of the revolution were outwardly calm. The appointment of a new Governor-General, Marcel-Edmond Naegelen, who enjoyed great popularity with the French community in Algeria, reassured the 'colons'. The Muslim opposition parties were preoccupied with their own internal organisation. But there were several signs that the situation was not happy. Changes were taking place in the Arab world. 1952 saw the emergence of Nasser. The Muslim Algerians could see the independence movements gathering strength in Tunisia and Morocco. The economic plan for Algeria was making only a slight impression on the country. The inequalities in wealth, and the growing Muslim population crowding wretchedly in the bidonvilles, or shanty towns, were a continual reminder of grievances. The Paris government, or succession of governments, were engaged with their own problems and felt that Algeria had been pacified by the passing of the Statute.

On All Saints night, 1 November 1954, armed attacks took place against police and guard-posts and public buildings. The Berber area of the Aurès was the scene of the greatest violence. Ten Frenchmen were killed in action, evoking a deep response from their compatriots both in France and Algeria. The Governor-General, alarmed at their protest, and at the degree of co-ordination that marked the original attacks, responded with harsh measures of repression and the arrest of at least 2000 members of political parties. The latter were now banding together in a Front de Libération Nationale (FLN), believing that 'le Mouvement National a atteint sa phase finale de réalisation'.[27] The liberal Mendès-France government in Paris decided to appoint Jacques Soustelle, at this stage not the uncomprising assimilationist he later became, to restore

Algeria to order and to supervise the carrying out of the 1947 Statute in its entirety.

La politique algérienne du Gouvernement [he wrote] ce que j'en savais ne semblait pas différer beaucoup de mes propres idées. Mitterand me précisa son position; lutte contre la rébellion en évitant à la fois toute faiblesse et tout excès; mise au point de l'Algérie de réformes; maintien intransigeant de l'Algérie dans le cadre français; accélération de l'évolution déjá commencée dans le sens d'une pleine accession des Musulmans aux fonctions et aux responsabilités. Le Gouvernement, ajoutait-on, me ferait largement confiance, et pour penser et pour agir.[28]

In June 1955 he announced his plan of moderate reform.[29] It stressed the word 'integration' but as an ethnographer, Soustelle also emphasised 'l'originalité ethnique, linguistique, religieuse de l'Algérie'. His aim was to identify Algeria completely with a French province, with electoral equality between the two peoples. He also wanted to improve the quality and effectiveness of the administration in rural areas. His suggestions pleased neither the nationalists, who felt that they had heard it all before, nor the *colons* who thought that the Governor-General was weakly giving in to nationalist violence.

The revolt sparked into life again. Massacres of Frenchmen at Ain Abid and al-Halia were countered by the execution of Muslims in the stadium at Philippeville. The United Nations debated the Algerian question but the French delegation questioned its competence to deal with an area which formed part of metropolitan France, and withdrew from the debate and from all other committees. The General Assembly, in face of this protest, abandoned the discussions. The apparent irresponsibility of the Muslims in organising so much violence in Algeria probably gained France supporters in the UN. At the beginning of 1956 a Republican Front came into power in Paris after the elections, with Guy Mollet, a socialist, as Prime

Minister.[30] He had fought the election on the slogan 'peace in Algeria', but a visit to Algiers where he was bitterly heckled by the *colons* led to a modification of his views. The candidate he had chosen for Governor-General, the moderate General Catroux, was replaced by Robert Lacoste, pledged to carry out Mollet's promises of a cease-fire, elections and then negotiations, *le triptych* as it became known ironically. Lacoste made little headway. Mollet had announced on his return from Algiers that 'les liens unissant la France métropolitane et l'Algérie étaient indissolubles' and in the sphere of practical administration Lacoste declared his firmness: 'Quant aux fanatiques aveugles, si leur folie fratricide ne cesse pas, ils apprendront à leurs dépens que la France frappe d'autant plus fort qu'elle a conscience d'être juste.'[31] His words were backed by an increase in French forces.

Opinion hardened on all sides in 1957. The army took a greater share in suppressing violence; parachute troops, *les paras*, took over Algiers. Their sympathy with the *colons* and their determination to prevent further humiliations to the army and to the French after the war in Indo-China led them to feel they had a political role as well as a military one. The Governor-General was by-passed, and the weakening Fourth Republic in France could do little to assert its authority over a situation which was affecting France itself. In Paris *les plastiquers* were demonstrating with their home-made bombs. The FLN was now committed to open rebellion until they gained complete independence. The Bandung Conference of 1955 had made it aware of African and Asian sympathy for the movement, while the granting of independence to Tunisia and Morocco emphasised the fact that the new Union française had little to offer to Algeria. Bitterness was increased by the arrest of Ben Bella, achieved by subterfuge in December 1956. The organisation of the party had improved with the development of revolutionary action. The Army of National

Liberation was backed by support of arms from Egypt as well as from its immediate neighbours. Its effectiveness became more and more apparent in the earlier part of 1958 when French casualties rose as high as 1000 in one week.

The *colons* were increasingly disillusioned with the policy evolved in Paris. The Gaillard government passed a *loi-cadre* in February 1958 respecting *la personnalité algérienne* and promised equal electoral rights in all the assemblies of the Republic.[32] M. Pflimlin's government which replaced it two months later appeared to the *colons* to ignore the immediacy of the Algerian problem and spoke only of 'negotiations' in the future. Backed by the army, the *colons* decided to form their own revolutionary government on 13 May. They sacked the offices of the Governor-General and set up Committees of Public Safety. General Massu headed the movement, the ultimate aim of which was to bring General de Gaulle back to power. General Massu's public statement in the Forum made this clear: 'Nous faisons appel au Général de Gaulle, seul capable de prendre la tête d'un gouvernement de Salut public, au-dessus de tous les partis, pour assurer la pérennité de l'Algérie française, partie intégrante de la France.'[33]

The response of General de Gaulle to such demands for his return is well known. On 4 June 1958, three days after he took over power, he visited Algiers and declared to the large French and Muslim crowd waiting for him, 'Je vous ai compris'. This enigmatic approach continued for the next year, and has induced critics to deny that de Gaulle had any Algerian policy whatsoever when he came to power.[34] It has led others to criticise also the timing and methods of the General's actions. A final judgment is as yet premature, but it is clear that General de Gaulle's position in France was not secure for some months and he had to tread warily for there was no easy solution in Algeria. No doubt he still hoped to retain some standing for

O. A. Salan

the *colons*, although 'L'Algérie de papa est passé'. His immediate action was to reduce the control of the army over the administration and to put forward social schemes to improve Muslim standards of living. On 16 September 1959 he felt able to say to the French nation on television that the choice lay among three courses of action, complete secession, integration or federation. 'Le sort des Algériens appartient aux Algériens, non point comme le leur imposeraient le couteau et la mitraillette, mais suivant la volonté qu'ils exprimeront légitimement par le suffrage universal. Avec eux et pour eux la France assurera la liberté de leur choix.'[35]

Supporters of Algérie française felt that they had been betrayed and engineered a second revolt in Algiers, 'the revolt of the barricades' in January 1960. De Gaulle's suppression of the insurrection put the Paris government more firmly in control of the Algerian situation than they had been since the outbreak of the revolution. Events still moved too slowly for the FLN but more particularly for the *colon* right wing in Algiers. A referendum of January 1961 with its vote of confidence for de Gaulle persuaded some army officers in Algeria that they had to fight to prevent an Algerian republic. The revolt of the colonels in April 1961 was put down, but it did not end the army's interference in politics. A month later General de Gaulle met the FLN leaders at Evian. The talks were inconclusive, but France had recognised the right of the FLN to negotiate with a sovereign state.

The President's claim that he could solve the Algerian problem seemed on the point of failure. The Organisation de l'armée secrète (OAS) became active both in France and Algeria and had the support of Generals Salan, Challe and Jouhaud. 'Trois ans pour choisir entre la valise et le cercueil, voilà le résultat de trois ans de politique gaulliste' ran one of their posters. Disillusionment with what they considered was a betrayal of France and Algérie française caused their last-ditch stand. But their extremism, and the violent measures they countenanced, alienated majority opinion in France, and prepared French opinion for the final agreement with the FLN at the second Evian meeting. This provided for a cease-fire, followed by a referendum on self-determination. It laid down that the French in Algeria could retain their nationality, and arrangements were made for Franco-Algerian co-operation in the future.

North Africa had gained its independence from France, but now had to face the problems of its own government. Once the unity of opposition to foreign rule had collapsed the new governments had to come to terms with the conflicting views of their own supporters. They had to define their position with France and the West, and also to decide what attitude they should take to the rest of the Arab world, and to the non-aligned countries of Africa.

NOTES TO CHAPTER 6
1. Julien, pp. 23–4.
2. A. H. Hourani, *Arabic Thought in the Liberal Age* (London, 1962), pp. 306–7.

3. Robert Murphy, *Diplomat among Warriors* (London, 1964), pp. 216–17.
4. Trans. from document in Le Tourneau, p. 209.
5. Julien, p. 355.
6. Trans. from Allal al-Fassi, *The Independence Movements in Arab North Africa* (Washington, 1954), p. 275.
7. Le Tourneau, p. 229.
8. Ibid. p. 247.
9. Julien, p. 95.
10. Le Tourneau, p. 109.
11. Julien, p. 180.
12. Ibid. pp. 182–5.
13. Le Tourneau, pp. 117–18.
14. H. Bourguiba, *La Tunisie et la France* (Paris, 1954), pp. 200–5.
15. Le Tourneau, p. 118.
16. J. Rous, *Tunisie . . . attention!* (Paris, 1952), p. 108.
17. Julien, p. 193 and Le Tourneau, pp. 120–1.
18. Le Tourneau, p. 119.
19. Rous, op. cit. pp. 119–22.
20. Le Tourneau, pp. 125–31.
21. Ibid. p. 134.
22. Murphy, op. cit. pp. 157–8.
23. Le Tourneau, p. 340.
24. Dorothy Pickles, *Algeria and France: from Colonialism to Co-operation* (London, 1963), pp. 26–7.
25. Le Tourneau, pp. 368–83.
26. Ibid. pp. 359–68.
27. Their full programme is printed in Le Tourneau, pp. 386–8.
28. Jacques Soustelle, *Aimée et souffrante Algérie* (Paris, 1956), p. 4.
29. Le Tourneau, pp. 394–7.
30. Pickles, op. cit. p. 35.
31. Le Tourneau, p. 406.
32. Ibid. p. 425.
33. A Debatty, *Le 13 Mai et la Presse* (Paris, 1960), p. 67.
34. See the debate in Pickles, op. cit. Ch. 6 pp. 120–60.
35. J. Soustelle, op. cit. Annexe iii, p. 273.

7 The Way to Suez

POST-WAR experiences in Palestine, Syria and Lebanon showed Britain and France that times were changing in the Middle East. The withdrawal of France from the Levant and her preoccupation with her internal stability and her North African empire left Britain alone in the area. In spite of the loss of India, the route through the Canal was now important for the preservation of Commonwealth links and trade, and for the passage of oil tankers. The oil industry, still in its infancy in 1939, had grown lustily in the latter part of the war, and international demands for its products had developed proportionately.[1] Although oil, by this stage, was an international concern rather than a purely British one, the protection of her interests was a powerful motive in determining policy. The great development of the Iraq fields and their vulnerable tentacles, the pipelines to the Mediterranean, made her anxious to see stable régimes in Iraq and Syria.

The British Labour Party and its Foreign Minister, Ernest Bevin, had surprised many of their supporters by their traditional Middle Eastern policy, but there was a hope that once the incubus of the Palestine Mandate had been removed a new era of good relations might begin. The changing political scene in the Middle East, however, made it difficult to ally with countries whose new governments were coming to power on a wave of anti-imperialist demonstrations. Syria witnessed 'a succession of military coups [which] gave control to army dictators allied to radical politicians'.[2] King Abdullah of Jordan, the traditional friend of Britain, was murdered in Jerusalem. The new kingdom forged out of traditional Jordan and the new acquisition of Arab Palestine was learning political views quickly.

In Iraq the wartime anti-British coup of 1941 was soon replaced by the restoration of the friendly Nuri es-Said. His retirement in 1944 led to renewed Iraqi demands for a revision of the 1930 Treaty. Britain was very anxious to retain Iraq's support and had been pouring money into the country with what *The Times* alleged to be 'almost quixotic generosity in view of the foreign exchange position in which this country now finds itself. The answer to that is no doubt that . . . Iraq would face an economic crisis if substantial amounts were not released. . . . For many reasons a crisis in Iraq would be unwelcome.'³ In January 1948 a new treaty was signed by Bevin and the Iraqi delegates at Portsmouth.⁴ The unpopular British Military Mission was replaced by an Anglo-Iraqi Joint Defence Board, and arrangements were made for joint defence projects. Iraqi negotiators accepted the terms with enthusiasm, but their reception on their return to Baghdad was less cordial. Rioting broke out and fifteen students were killed. At their funeral more demonstrations took place. 'A six-mile procession was led by political and religious leaders and the coffins were covered with huge flags and bore large letters written in the blood of the victims. Thousands of people brandished swords, knives and revolvers, and carried banners inscribed with "Victims for freedom and independence", "You died so that the Iraqi people could live", and "We want the heads of Salih Jabr, Nuri es-Said, and their henchmen".'⁵ The Portsmouth proposals were dropped, but although the violent opposition to them showed the strength of nationalist feeling in Iraq, there was no break with Britain. The politicians, sobered by the military defeat of the Arabs in Palestine, were anxious not to go too far.

In Aden and the Gulf relations were as yet uncomplicated,

Sir Charles Belgrave was still secure in his paternal role of adviser to the Sheikh of Bahrain, a post which he had held from 1926.[6] Only the beginning of the dispute over Buraimi, the chief oasis in northern Oman, was a cloud in the sky. Its importance increased by American oil discoveries in 1949, it became a bone of contention between Britain, who was the protector of the Sultan of Oman, and Saudi Arabia. The question was eventually referred to international arbitration, another indication that Britain could no longer decide issues on her own.[7]

Further north in Iran British policy, fortified by her experiences in the Second World War, was to support an independent Iran with a strong central government, free from foreign interference, particularly that of Soviet Russia. Throughout the war Britain was represented by Sir Reader Bullard in Teheran. 'Intelligent and erudite, firm and yet friendly, [he] personified in his simple and unassuming manner all the best traditions of British diplomacy.'[8] His presence did much to uphold the reputation of his country against the propaganda of the Soviet Union. The country suffered from the disruption of its oil supplies in the first two years of the war, and then began producing increased supplies to meet the demands of war and peace. In 1947 a pipeline was built from the Gulf to the Mediterranean. The oilfields and the refinery were modernised. The Iranian Government became discontented with their share of royalties which they alleged were not as great as the United States allowed their South American companies, so in July 1949 a supplemental agreement was drawn up with the Anglo-Iranian Oil Company.[9] The new arrangement gave the Iranians a revenue increased by 50 per cent.

But this did not satisfy the growing feeling of nationalism in Iran. The protest which 'began as a movement against the Anglo-Iranian Oil Company although it was anti-foreign in form in the early period . . . was a reflection in the main of the discontent with the ruling classes, of the disequilibrium in political, social and economic affairs inside Persia, and of the fear that dictatorship would be re-imposed with foreign support.'[10] Dr Musaddiq and the National Front took up the nationalisation of oil as part of their programme. The Prime Minister, Ali Razmara, who suggested that his countrymen could not manage to run their own industry, was murdered, and when Dr Musaddiq succeeded him in office, the industry was nationa-lised and violent anti-British demonstrations took place.

The histrionic Musaddiq won much popularity by an American television appearance which drew world attention to his struggle against imperialist Britain. In Britain itself party conflict arose over the issue. The Conservative opposition criticised the Labour Cabinet for their policy of 'scuttle'.[11] By the end of 1951 all the British technical staff had left Abadan. The dispute, so harmful to Iran's prosperity, was not settled until 1954 when an international consortium agreement was drawn up in which Britain took part. The incident showed the Middle East how easy it now was to twist the lion's tail, and how far a nationalist movement would go in harming its own economy to do so. For Britain it proved how helpless she was to protect her interests with force in the post-war world, but the lesson of self-restraint in 1951 was lost on the Conservative politicians of 1956.

THE COLD WAR IN THE MIDDLE EAST

Churchill's speech in Fulton, Missouri, in March 1946, which put into words the growing fears of Russian aggres-sion, ushered in the era of the 'Cold War'. The Middle East became one of the battlefields in the struggle. As Britain had done most of the fighting on this front during the war Russia could not make any open intervention. She had to act by means of her ideological propaganda which was likely to appeal to many elements in the under-developed countries of the Middle East. The Western powers could act in a more open way by forming alliances and securing bases.

Bevin realised in the early days of Britain's financial difficulties that the country could not bear the whole burden of defence arrangements in the area. The United States was asked to help in the protection of Greece and Turkey. The American Secretary of the Navy Forrestal noted wryly in his diary: 'Marshall said that this dumped in our lap another most serious problem ... that it was tantamount to British abdication from the Middle East with obvious implications as to their successor.'[12] The United States accepted the commitment, and the Truman Doctrine, proclaimed on 12 March, 1947, concentrated on Greece and Turkey as the potential sources of danger.[13] 'It is necessary only to glance at a map to realise that the survival and integrity of the Greek nation are of grave importance in a much wider situation. If Greece should fall under the control of an armed minority, the effect upon its neighbour Turkey would be immediate and serious. Confusion and disorder might well spread throughout the entire Middle East.' This thinking led to the inclusion of the two countries in the North Atlantic Treaty Organisation, formed in 1949.

A scheme to form a Middle East Defence Organisation in 1951 was not successful, because Egypt regarded it with suspicion as a new form of colonialism.[14] The United States, realising that motives might be questioned, began to sponsor military and economic aid rather than to insist on active participation. In 1953 Mr Dulles suggested that more attention should be paid to the danger of the 'Northern Tier' states, those which lay nearest to Russia. Turkey and Pakistan signed a treaty of friendship in April 1954. At the beginning of the following year, in February 1955, Turkey and Iraq made a pact of mutual co-operation (the Baghdad Pact) which was later joined by Britain, Pakistan and Iran.[15]

The Arabs regarded it with extreme hostility as an attempt
to split the Arab League by isolating Iraq.

THE EGYPTIAN REVOLUTION

It still seemed to Britain that Egypt was the main source of
anxiety in the area. After the loss of Palestine plans were
again concentrated on making sure that a base could be
kept in the country. This appeared to Britain particularly
important because of the political situation within Egypt
itself. By the early fifties all the ruling groups were dis-
credited. The dissolute King Farouk, led by a palace
coterie, continued to act arbitrarily. The Wafd Party, the
nucleus of opposition to British influence before the war,
was succumbing to lethargy and bribery, the occupational
diseases of Egyptian politicians. The zealous activities of
the Muslim Brotherhood, who advocated the expulsion of
foreign elements and a return to the tenets of Islam as the
only way of solving the problems of twentieth-century
Egypt, had won them over a million members by 1952. But
their anarchical methods added to the general bankruptcy
of political life.

In 1952 it was an army junta who organised a bloodless
coup d'état which overthrew the King and the constitution.
The first two years under 'amiable, pipe-smoking, fatherly'
General Neguib were a period of conservative consolida-
tion.[16] Gamal Abdel Nasser and the younger officers were
not content with an incomplete revolution. Egyptian defeat
in the Palestine war was the spark that ignited their movement, but behind it lay years of political planning.[17] Gamal
Abdel Nasser, only thirty-four years old when he took over
from Neguib in 1954, had been trained at the Military
Academy in Cairo, and had had military experience in the
Sudan as well as in Palestine. In 1950 he had become
president of the committee of Free Officers, a revolutionary
group who wanted to remodel Egyptian society. Nasser's

'Philosophy of the Revolution' did not contain a detailed plan of what he wanted to achieve. His ideas were clarified slowly in response to the difficulties he faced in Egypt and abroad, and the development of his own political experience. He inherited first and foremost the serious economic problem of every Egyptian ruler from the time of Muhammad Ali, a rapidly growing population in a country that had little fertile land. The curbing of the landlords, the education of a backward people, the introduction of social and health measures, all of which had scarcely been touched in the period of British administration, also demanded immediate attention.

The British Government, now Conservative with Anthony Eden as Foreign Secretary, hoped that the new Egyptian régime would re-open talks. One difficulty at least was removed in February 1953 by the signing of an Agreement between Britain and the Sudan which gave the country independence after a transitional period.[18] The problem of the land base remained between Britain and Egypt. Talks began in 1953 and were continued in the following year, each step needing careful deliberation on both sides, after the unilateral renunciation of the 1936 Treaty by Egypt in 1951. Finally, on 19 October 1954 the new agreement was signed.[19] The British Government accepted the termination of the 1936 Treaty. British troops were to be 'completely withdrawn from Egyptian territory . . . within a period of twenty months from the date of signature of the present Agreement'. There was the proviso, however, that 'in the event of an armed attack by an outside Power on any country which . . . is a party to the Treaty of Joint Defence between Arab League States, signed in Cairo on the 13th April 1950, or on Turkey, Egypt still offered to the United Kingdom such facilities as may be necessary in order to place the Base on a war footing and to operate it effectively.' Nasser had won his first diplomatic success, and his popularity grew inside Egypt.

FRANCE AND ISRAEL

Meanwhile, Israel was also facing the problems of the 1948–9 War, and the creation of a new State in a hostile Middle East. A United Nations Conciliation Commission (PCC) was set up in December 1948 'to take steps to assist the Governments and authorities concerned to achieve a final settlement of all questions outstanding between them'.[20] Its terms of reference were impossible to carry out because Arabs refused to meet Israelis; the Lausanne 'conference' of 1949 foundered on this rock. The Commission admitted its failure two years later but it was not dissolved. In Jerusalem the checkpoint at the Mandelbaum Gate, between the Israeli and Jordanian zone, was a perpetual reminder of the divisions of the city. By the end of 1949 the Israeli Government had moved its capital from Tel Aviv to Jerusalem. Chaim Weizmann became President of the new State; a Parliament, the Knesset, was set up and David Ben Gurion became first Prime Minister.

Israel was boycotted economically by the Arab States and this threw her more into the arms of the West. United States aid poured into the country, and the capital provided, together with the dedication of its people, helped to develop the country. The early successes of the *kibbutzim*, or agricultural co-operatives, made even the Negev desert fruitful. But Israel needed military protection in the perpetual anxiety of her position. This demand found a response in France, who had left the Levant in 1945 disillusioned with the Arabs. A certain number of French arms had found their way to help the Haganah in the Arab-Israeli war, and although France had been slow to recognise the new State because she did not want to provoke the opposition of the Arab bloc in the United Nations against her North African policy, there was a fund of sympathy for the Israelis.[21]

The appointment of a new ambassador to Israel, Pierre-Eugène Gilbert, in April 1953, began a conscious effort to build up pro-French sentiment in Israel.[22] Self-interest was involved on both sides. The French, attacked by the Arab League and fearing its propaganda in North Africa, welcomed an alliance in the Middle East. Israel felt she could benefit from the link in three ways; commercial dealings with France, the purchase of armaments, and the exchange of scientific research.

The ties appear to have become stronger by the summer of 1953.[23] Israel had been able to offer a cheaper process for producing heavy water for France's nuclear programme, and in return Israel negotiated for delivery of aircraft and arms. In August 1954, Moshe Dayan made an official visit to Paris. 'L'amitié franco-israélienne, discrète dans le passé, entre avec cette visite dans une ère de rapprochement affirmé à la face du monde, le monde arabe y compris.'[24] At the end of the same year, 1954, the first Ouragan fighters were delivered to Israel.

THE ARAB-ISRAELI QUARREL

The state of war existing between the Arabs and Israel expressed itself in every sphere of interest. As well as refusing to trade with the Israelis, the Arabs tried to blacklist ships which called at Israeli ports, and refused overflying rights to aeroplanes which landed at Israeli airports on their way to and from the Far East. Israeli ships were prevented from using the Suez Canal. Britain felt that little could be done for Israel as the two States were technically at war, but she raised the issue at the United Nations. In September 1951 the Security Council ordered Egypt to allow Israeli vessels through the Canal on the grounds that the Egyptian sanctions represented 'unjustified interference with the rights of nations to navigate the seas and to trade freely with one another, including the Arab states and Israel'.[25] Neither this injunction nor a further UN censure in 1954 was heeded by the Egyptians. The Israeli merchant ship *Bat Galim* sent through the Canal later in 1954 as a test case was confiscated, and her crew imprisoned. International opinion ignored the incident. A Russian veto in the Security Council in March 1954 prevented the Israelis from protesting about the Egyptian guns at Sharm el-Sheikh which threatened their port at Eilat on the Gulf of Aqaba.[26]

Throughout these years the Arab refugee problem exacerbated Arab-Israeli relations still further. Britain and France joined to help in the relief of hunger and disease, but resettlement of the majority of the refugees was impossible. Israel rejected them on the ground that they would be better off in their own cultural surroundings; the Arabs wanted to keep the problem alive as a propaganda weapon. Some refugees joined the bands of *fedayeen*, or guerrilla raiders who had crossed the frontier from Egypt to Israel from the time of the 1948-9 war. Arms were needed both for these border raids, and for the open war that both Egypt and Israel expected would come. The Western Powers had foreseen this arms race, and in May 1950 Britain, France and the United States had signed a Tripartite Declaration.[27] The three governments said that 'Should they find that any of these States was prepared to violate frontiers or armistice lines, [they] would consistent with their obligations as members of the United Nations, immediately take action both within and outside the United Nations to prevent such violation.' The threat hung over Egypt and Israel for the next five years, but did not prevent the building up of armaments on both sides. Israel's requests to France have already been discussed; Egypt turned towards the Soviet bloc and in 1955 concluded an agreement with Czechoslovakia for a delivery of armaments on the security of the cotton crop.

THE WAY TO SUEZ

Although foreign affairs played their part in Nasser's policy in his first years of office and had strengthened his leadership, he realised that he would stand or fall on the success of his economic measures at home. The idea of building a High Dam at Aswan was conceived to irrigate a much larger area of the country, and to provide a livelihood and homes for more people in Upper Egypt. Nasser sought help from Western governments for the enterprise. Initially he obtained promises of $55 million from the United States, and $15 million from Britain, and then $200 million from the World Bank after the other offers were forthcoming. On 15 July 1956 the United States withdrew her offer, closely followed by the other two guarantors.

What motives lay behind this reversal of policy? The United States appears to have become apprehensive about the *rapprochement* of Egypt and the Communist bloc. In May Egypt had recognised Communist China, and a month later the Russian Foreign Minister, Shepilov, visited Cairo and was reputed to have offered a large loan without interest. Robert Murphy, Eisenhower's special adviser, commented later:

Those of us who worked with Dulles were never told explicitly why he acted so abruptly. We surmised that perhaps the main reason was because Nasser was scheduled to make a trip to Moscow early in August. If the United States would agree to the Aswan Dam financing, the Egyptian President could then concentrate in Moscow on concluding his second big arms deal with the Russians, thus getting the best of both worlds.'[28]

The President of the World Bank had also become worried about Nasser's intentions.

Britain had already began to have doubts about her own financial commitments in the scheme. 'There was not only a limit to what we could afford', the Prime Minister wrote later. 'We had also to take account of the position of our allies, notably Iraq, who had their own needs.'[29] Although the 1948 Portsmouth negotiations had come to nothing, a special agreement was drawn up on 4 April 1955 between Britain and Iraq to 'maintain and develop peace and friendship between their two countries'.[30] Nuri es-Said in Baghdad felt that the Iraqi régime could not last unless Nasser were held in check. Jordan was also smarting under the whip of Nasser's propaganda. In October 1955 General Templer, Chief of the British Imperial General Staff, was sent to Amman to encourage Jordan to join the Baghdad Pact. Riots shook the capital and brought down three successive governments, with the result that Jordan promised Egypt she would not yield to British pressure. In March 1956 Glubb Pasha was summarily dismissed from his position as adviser to the Jordanian Government. Nasser's hand was seen behind this action, although he later denied having any part in it.[31] There was, in fact, no reason why he should; King Hussein of Jordan himself wanted to show his independence from the tutelage of foreigners.

Anthony Eden had become British Prime Minister in succession to Churchill, in April 1955. Anthony Nutting, Minister of State at the Foreign Office in 1956, has discussed the Prime Minister's ill health and failing nerve at this important stage of his career.[32] He had been the 'Golden Boy' of the Conservative Party for too long, and was not prepared for the criticism he met when he had complete direction of the country's affairs. 'He was not a leader in the Churchillian tradition and nothing could ever make him so. He was a negotiator, a mediator *par excellence*.' The Glubb incident convinced him of Nasser's perfidy, and he saw in the Egyptian a new Hitler or Mussolini. He was not alone in being haunted by the 'Munich Spectre'. The French Prime Minister, Guy Mollet, also felt that Nasser's ideas were similar to those expressed in *Mein*

Kampf. Christian Pineau, the French Foreign Minister, returning from a visit to Cairo, reported later: 'He is not a second Hitler. He is a man without big [sic] political experience and I am sure that he will never be dictator of the Middle East. But Guy Mollet was not so sure as me of this impression.'³³ But in the spring of 1956 France and Egypt were still friendly because of their mutual dislike of the Baghdad Pact, and Pineau's Cairo visit was an attempt to get assurances that Nasser would not help the Algerians. Disillusionment with Egyptian promises led the French Prime Minister, and the Defence Minister, Bourgès-Manoury, to turn against Nasser completely by July 1956.

THE SUMMER OF 1956

Nasser's response to the withdrawal of funds for the High Dam was to nationalise the Suez Canal on 26 July 1956. In a speech in Alexandria on the anniversary of the revolution in Egypt, he pronounced 'a battle against imperialism and the methods and tactics of imperialism, and a battle against Israel, the vanguard of imperialism, which was created by imperialism in an effort to annihilate our nationalism in the same way as it annihilated Palestine.'³⁴ Egypt had taken part in the Bandung Conference of non-aligned African and Asian nations the year before, and as Nasser mentioned later in his speech, he felt he had a great deal of support behind him. Britain and France as Canal shareholders were deeply concerned with the Egyptian action, and seem to have discussed the use of force immediately. There was, in fact, no doubt that the Canal itself belonged to Egypt, but it was run by the Suez Canal Company in which the British and the French had controlling interests. The French middle class used the Canal shares as a common investment. Both powers also felt that the Egyptians could not run the Canal satisfactorily, although the Norwegians pointed out at a very early stage in the affair that the practical difficulties were not so great as was alleged.

Eden sent a cable to Eisenhower shortly after the nationalisation: 'My colleagues and I are convinced that we must be ready in the last resort to use force to bring Nasser to his senses.'[35] The United States urged caution. As a fellow signatory to the Tripartite agreement as well as a Canal user she was as concerned as the British and the French in the nationalisation of the Canal. Robert Murphy went to London 'to see what it was all about', dined with Harold Macmillan and 'was left in no doubt that the British Government believed that Suez was a test which could be met only by the use of force'.[36]

At the beginning of August the British Government invited the signatories to the 1888 Convention to a conference in London, 'to consider what steps could most appropriately be taken to establish operating arrangements under an international system designed to assure the continuity of operation of the Canal.'[37] On the same day, 2 August, there was a House of Commons debate on Suez in which a crack began to appear between the parties. Hugh Gaitskell, Leader of the Opposition, agreed with the determination to be firm with Nasser, but he felt that the United Nations should judge the issue. Eden was determined to keep it in British hands. On 8 August he made a broadcast speech to the nation, in which it was evident that the defeat of Nasser was uppermost in his mind. 'The pattern is familiar to many of us, my friends. We all know this is how fascist governments behave and we all remember, only too well, what the cost can be in giving in to fascism . . . with dictators you always have to pay a higher price later on, for their appetite grows with feeding.'[38]

Five days earlier, M. Pineau speaking in the French National Assembly had mentioned French fears at Nasser's action over the Canal, his support of the Algerian nationalists and his opposition to Israel. He called for a closer link with London. 'Si, aujourd'hui encore, nous insistons tellement sur cette necessité de la solidarité occidentale, c'est parce que toute la force de l'Egypte, au cours des six derniers mois, a reposé sur des divisions déplorables.'[39]

The result was an unexpected *rapprochement* between Britain and France, both of whom felt, for reasons already discussed, that Nasser must be overthrown and that a mere assurance about the Canal was not enough. The United States was not informed of their deeper purpose, although it became clearer as the weeks went by. France was ready to attack at once, but Britain was more hesitant, for she had more to lose in the Arab world by an armed attack. Both Hussein of Jordan and Nuri es-Said, the declared friends of Great Britain, opposed her on this issue, nor did Britain want to attack without United States backing, nor to forego her 'special relationship' with that country. So the opportunity for a surprise action went by.

Publically the fiction of negotiation was kept up. The first London Conference which met in August drew up a list of proposals for the international control of the Canal which Mr Menzies, the Australian Prime Minister, was to convey to President Nasser, because Egypt did not choose to attend. The Indian and Russian delegates put the Egyptian case in London. Menzies' mission was condemned to failure by Eisenhower's open declaration that 'the United States cannot, in any circumstances, support the use of force'. Meanwhile the Canal continued to work, and no Briton, nor Frenchman living in Egypt had his property harmed. Nasser made the suggestion that the Canal users should have a new treaty in return for payment of tolls to him. London rejected the idea, which would leave them without an excuse for military intervention, and began to plan an invasion. The 15 September was the first date suggested, because the Commander-in-Chief in the Middle East thought that military arrangements could be ready by that time, and the Canal Company announced that foreign pilots would be withdrawn on that date.

Meanwhile pressures were growing for a presentation of the Anglo-French case to the United Nations. The view held by a number of Commonwealth countries was presented by Mr Lester Pearson, Canadian Minister for External Affairs. The United States, under the strain of the forthcoming presidential election, became more impatient with the threats of war, and it was evident that the United States would not stand by without protesting if the European countries resorted to force. The personal gulf between Dulles and Eden widened.[40] At the beginning of September, the American Secretary of State had suggested a Suez Canal Users Association (SCUA). It was soon clear that Britain and the United States differed about the purpose of this 'club'. On 11 September, Eisenhower announced in answer to a press conference question that he 'would not be a party to agression', implying that France and Britain, not Nasser, were the aggressors. Two days later Dulles dropped his bombshell. At a press conference on the new Users Club, he revealed that the United States would not be prepared to support SCUA with force. 'I want to say right now that it is fantastic that anyone should wish to impose some undesirable régime on Egypt and we won't do it, certainly not as far as the United States is concerned. The association is not intended to guarantee anything to anybody.'[41] The split between Britain and the United States was complete.

THE LAST DAYS

Britain and France persisted with the idea of a Users Association, and its establishment was the main purpose of the second London Conference which ended on 21 September. The plan had been modified in the course of discussions and some delegates were prepared to accept the idea of paying tolls. Britain and France, deciding that matters were not going the way they wanted, at last put the matter before the Security Council, lest they should alienate international, and particularly American, opinion too far. On 5 October Mr Selwyn Lloyd asked for the support of SCUA. On 13 October the proposal was rejected by Russia's veto.

Meanwhile steps were being taken to involve Israel with the Anglo-French plans. The situation in Jordan was causing anxiety; there was to be an election on 21 October, and Nasser's propaganda among the Arab refugees was already having its effect. France was continuing her military and technical advice to Israel and on 23 September Shimon Peres, Israeli Head of Defence, was in Paris for talks. Pineau flew to London to interest Eden in co-operation between the three. As Pineau later stated, 'It was the first time I had brought up the possibility of Israeli collaboration with Eden and Lloyd. Their reaction was, at first, very subtle. Eden showed a great deal of interest, Lloyd a great deal of reticence.' Mr Lloyd's preoccupations seemed to be above all not to compromise Britain with regard to the Arab countries and not to run the risk of involving Britain's treaty obligations with Jordan. Never-theless, 'I was able to persuade them to give me a kind of *carte blanche* to undertake further negotiations with the Israelis and keep them up to date on developments.'[42] Israel, from her point of view, needed British Canberras based on Cyprus if she were to put Egyptian airfields out of action before the superior Russian Ilyushins, owned by the Egyptians, could attack her cities. Negotiations went on from here. On 16 October there was an important meeting in Paris between the British and French Prime Ministers and Foreign Ministers, where a more detailed timetable was worked out. On 23–24 October secret meetings took place in Sèvres on the outskirts of Paris. Here, according to later French and Israeli revelations, an actual treaty was signed by the three countries.[43] Israel was anxious to have Britain's written agreement of support.

The Israeli attack began on 29 October.* On the following day an ultimatum was handed to the Egyptian and Israeli ambassadors in London by the British and French Governments, saying that the two Middle Eastern states were to 'withdraw' to lines ten miles each side of the Canal, so that British and French troops could occupy the Canal Zone. Dayan, the Israeli commander, knew that it was a blind, but in any case it allowed the Israelis to advance on all fronts. Nasser rejected the peremptory demand.

The United Nations continued its debate, but Britain and France vetoed the Security Council's resolution asking all countries not to use force in the Middle East. In France the National Assembly supported Mollet with a vote of 368 to 182. In Britain the support for Eden was 270, but the vote did not prevent the growing uneasiness of the House. Egypt still felt that Eden was bluffing, but was convinced by the much delayed Allied bombing attack on Egyptian airfields on 31 October. Nasser withdrew his troops from Sinai to protect Cairo, and Israel took advantage of this retreat to complete her conquest of Gaza and Sharm el-Sheikh, the key position overlooking the Gulf of Aqaba. Ben Gurion would have been prepared to accept a cease-fire at this point as he was reluctant to antagonise the United Nations any further, but his Western allies persisted in their aim of 'knocking Nasser off his perch'. The Allied 'Operation Musketeer' was slow in execution, and it was not until 5 November that British and French paratroops were dropped near Port Said.

Bulganin, who had been preoccupied with Hungary, wrote irate notes to the invading powers and invited the

* The situation had been complicated by Israeli-Jordanian border attacks. At one point it looked as though Britain would be supporting Jordan against Israel, and at the same time fighting with Israel against Egypt.

United States to join him in negotiating a Middle Eastern settlement. Eisenhower declined; he wanted to stick to the United Nations Charter to the end. But pressures were increasing on all sides to stop the conflict, and on 6 November Britain called for a cease-fire. The war was over.

NOTES ON CHAPTER 7

1. For detailed facts and figures on the growth of the oil industry see bibliographical section on oil.
2. Monroe, p. 170.
3. George Kirk, *The Middle East, 1945–1950* (London, 1954), p. 153.
4. Treaty of Alliance between the U.K. and Iraq, Portsmouth 15 January, 1948. Cmd. 7309 (H.M.S.O. London, 1948).
5. Kirk, op. cit. p. 157, quoting *Manchester Guardian*, (29 January, 1948).
6. Sir Charles Belgrave, *Personal Column* (London, 1960).
7. The best book on the dispute is J. B. Kelly, *Eastern Arabian Frontiers* (London, 1964) David Holden gives a good summary in *Farewell to Arabia* (London, 1966), pp. 201–13.
8. George Lenezowski, *Russia and the West in Iran, 1918–1948* (Ithaca, New York, 1949), p. 256.
9. Hurewitz, ii, pp. 305–8.
10. Ann Lambton, 'The impact of the West on Persia', in *International Affairs*, Vol. 33 (January, 1957), p. 24.
11. F. S. Northedge, *British Foreign Policy* (London, 1962), p. 124.
12. 25 February, 1947. Walter Millis (ed.), *The Forrestal Diaries* (New York, 1951), p. 245.
13. Hurewitz, ii, pp. 273–5.
14. Ibid. pp. 329–32.
15. Ibid. pp. 390–1.
16. Peter Mansfield, *Nasser's Egypt* (London, 1965), pp. 44–5.
17. Gamal Abdel Nasser, *The Philosophy of the Revolution* (Cairo, 1954), pp. 12–15.

18. Hurewitz, ii, pp. 335–7.
19. Ibid. pp. 383–4.
20. Walter Eytan, *The First Ten Years. Israel between East and West* (London, 1958), p. 48.
21. Michel Bar-Zohar, *Suez Ultra Secret* (Paris, 1964), pp. 36–8.
22. Ibid. pp. 58–60.
23. Terence Robertson in Anthony Moncrieff (ed.), *Suez Ten Years After* (London, 1967), p. 61.
24. Comment in *Davar* (Tel-Aviv, 20.8.1954) quoted in Bar-Zohar, op. cit. p. 70.
25. Quoted in W. Eytan, op. cit. p. 94.
26. The Israeli point of view in this issue can be followed in the speeches of Abba Eban, Israel's ambassador to the UN, *Voice of Israel* (London, 1958), pp. 202–18. On the refugee question, pp. 168–86.
27. Hurewitz, ii, pp. 308–11.
28. Robert Murphy, *Diplomat among Warriors* (London, 1964), p. 459.
29. Sir Anthony Eden, *Full Circle* (London, 1960), p. 421.
30. Hurewitz, ii, pp. 391–5.
31. Gamal Abdel Nasser, in Moncrieff, op. cit. p. 34.
32. Anthony Nutting, *No End of a Lesson: the Story of Suez* (London, 1967), pp. 17–27.
33. Christian Pineau, in Moncrieff, op. cit. p. 35.
34. *D.I.A. 1956*, p. 80.
35. Murphy, op. cit. p. 461.
36. Ibid. p. 463.
37. *D.I.A. 1956*, p. 140.
38. Ibid. pp. 158–61.
39. Ibid. pp. 140–50.
40. The role of Dulles in the Suez affair has been the subject of much discussion. See the books of Finer, Murphy, Robertson and Nutting for different views.
41. Terence Robertson, *Crisis: the Inside Story of the Suez Conspiracy* (London, 1965), p. 118.
42. Ibid. p. 135.
43. See appendix on the Historiography of Suez.

8 The Years after Suez

THE brief Suez war was over, but the problems it raised remained. In spite of the independent action of two of its most eminent members, the United Nations emerged to a greater strength than it had shown hitherto.[1] It had been unable to enforce the armistice terms after the 1948–9 Arab–Israeli war, but now the Canadian Foreign Minister Lester Pearson's plan for a peace-keeping force was adopted. The United Nations force would remain to keep the warring powers away from each other's throats, without insisting on disarmament first. 'Without pretending to either the punitive or the enforcing function of an army, it was yet going beyond the exhortations, the protests, the resolutions of the conference table. It was inserting itself non-violently but yet physically, visibly, tangibly into a situation which mere diplomacy could not resolve. . . .'[2] When the nations concerned accepted the idea of United Nations' action, the peace-keeping force moved in, and by 22 December the evacuation of British troops was completed.

Why had Britain given in so quickly? Eden himself put the view that once Israeli and Egyptian fighting was over, British action had to stop too. 'We had intervened to divide and, above all, to contain the conflict. The occasion for our intervention was over, the fire was out.'[3] Later critics have seen a more forcible argument in the run on sterling, and the possibility of the devaluation of the pound.[4] The United States refused to back the pound while the war continued, but the International Monetary Fund, supported by the United States Government, promised a loan of £300

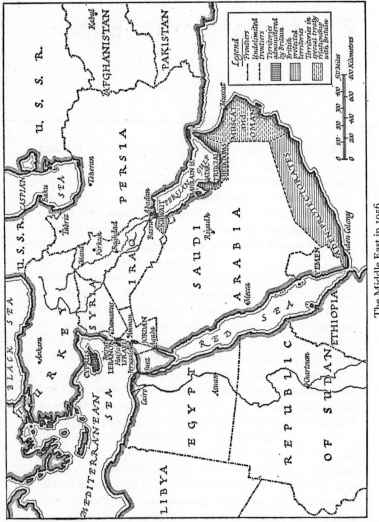

The Middle East in 1956

millions if there were a cease-fire by midnight on 6 November.[5] Harold Macmillan, the Chancellor of the Exchequer,
appears to have been influenced by this argument to back
down from the earlier warlike fervour reported by Robert
Murphy.[6] Eden, exhausted by ill health, was also persuaded
by hostile criticism from abroad and fear of divisions within
the Cabinet.[7] Alarm at the prospect of Russian attacks on
the West seemed to carry less weight.[8] Nor did public
outcry in Britain have much effect; in fact opinion polls
showed that Eden had a majority, if only a small majority,
in favour of his Middle East policy.[9]

The withdrawal marked the end of the brief *entente*
between Britain and France. The latter was reluctant to
accept the cease-fire, and had it not been for the practical
difficulties of continuing the war, she might have supported
Israel in a longer campaign.[10] She felt that the military
withdrawal was a humiliation, and she blamed Britain for
lacking the courage of her convictions, but she was less
guilt-ridden than her ally and recovered more quickly. She
had little influence left to lose in the Middle East; her
concern was with Algeria rather than the Canal, and by
13 June 1957 her ships were using the Canal, and paying
their tolls to the Egyptian government.

Israel, although she too would have liked to continue the
invasion, had proved her military capabilities, both to her
own citizens and to outsiders. As a practical result, the
fedayeen raids on her borders had ceased and she could use
the port of Eilat. Moshe Dayan, Israel's Commander-in-
Chief, expressed the main Israeli satisfaction in the outcome
of the war: 'The main change in the situation achieved by
Israel, however, was manifested among her Arab neighbours. Israel's readiness to take to the sword to secure her
rights at sea and her safety on land, and the capacity of her
army to defeat the Egyptian forces, deterred the Arab
rulers in the years that followed from renewing their acts
of hostility.'[11]

Nasser, in spite of military defeat, gained most from the incident. The sympathies of Russia and the non-aligned world were with him. His control over the nationalised Canal was established, with its tolls coming into the Egyptian exchequer once it had been cleared of sunken ships and was working satisfactorily under new Egyptian managers. Nasser's position as a leader in the Arab world was recognised. He began to support subversive activities throughout the Orient, attacking the British and French positions and decrying the pro-Western régimes in Iraq and Jordan. Later his activities spread to Tunisia, Libya, Lebanon and Saudi Arabia. In the years after the Suez war Nasser and Arab unity almost became identified. The Syrian Ba'ath Socialist Party which also had plans for unifying the Arab world[12] turned to him as the man most likely to achieve this aim, and in February 1958 Egypt and Syria joined in a single centralised state, the United Arab Republic. It was a positive step towards a larger union of Arab countries.

THE 1958 CRISIS

Britain had lost all round in the Suez débâcle. Her prestige and influence in the Arab world were destroyed completely.[13] She had forfeited respect in the Commonwealth and damaged her alliance with the United States. The way seemed open for the event most feared in the Middle East after the end of the Second World War, the more direct participation of the Soviet Union in the area, particularly when the launching of the first Sputnik showed her technical superiority. But Anthony Eden had been replaced as Prime Minister by Harold Macmillan, who healed many of the wounds his party had suffered. 'Suez, like Gallipoli, was a great destroyer of reputations – military as well as political. It is often forgotten that it made others. The new toryism that Mr Macmillan created between 1957 and 1960 was born out of the post-Suez shambles.'[14] One of the cornerstones of this policy was a close *rapprochement* with the United States.

The Americans themselves felt that the ill-timed action of Britain at Suez put a greater emphasis on their role in the Middle East, and they attempted to evolve a policy which would meet these new obligations. The Eisenhower Doctrine was announced on 31 December 1956, and was at once put into action.[15] It declared that any Russian intervention in the area would at once be met by the United States, with force if all else failed. Between 400 and 500 million dollars were to be spent on a programme of aid in the two years following the announcement.

United States involvement was put to the test in 1958.[16] On 14 July King Feisal of Iraq and Nuri es-Said were murdered, the monarchy was overthrown and a republic under General Kassem set up. The Middle East situation appeared to be once more on the point of conflagration. Nasser's propaganda was spreading and there was a danger that other countries might overthrow their governments. President Chamoun of Lebanon, who tried to amend the constitution, was strongly opposed by the Muslim group of the community; he had also refused to break off relations with Britain and France in 1956, and was criticised for a too subservient policy to the West. He appealed to the United States for help. The United States Sixth Fleet landed troops on the Lebanese beaches where they did little more than buy Coca-Cola from enthusiastic Lebanese vendors, but the situation was frozen for a period, and the civil war in the delicately balanced religious and political situation of Lebanon was averted. British paratroops were sent at the same time in answer to an appeal from King Hussein of Jordan, and here too the threat to the monarchy was averted. But the incidents had shown that Anglo-American activities had really very little effect on Middle Eastern politics.

On 19 July Chairman Khruschev suggested a meeting of the USSR, the United States, Britain, France, India and the Secretary-General of the United Nations to discuss the Middle Eastern situation. He was amiably willing to alter times and places to suit the Western powers, and he refrained from antagonising them by inviting President Nasser to be one of the number. But no one was anxious to admit Russia's right to take part in any such discussion. De Gaulle objected to the inclusion of the United Nations representative, and wanted any discussions, if they were to take place, to be in Europe. Britain also declined to take part in so large a gathering.

The United States realised that the Eisenhower Doctrine was not working well. Nasser's influence was still strong, and the State Department decided that a strong Egypt was perhaps the most valuable asset in the Middle East.[17] The business of trying to win the Arabs over to the American point of view had merely driven them more firmly towards arms deals with the Soviet Union, therefore on 13 August 1958 President Eisenhower appeared before the General Assembly of the United Nations, and put forward a plea for Arab isolationism and non-alignment with any great power. Their neutrality would be protected by the United Nations. Shortly afterwards Secretary-General Hammarskjöld made a tour of the Middle East, and foreign troops were removed from Lebanon and Jordan. The new confidence seemed justified. Kassem's Iraqi régime joined neither the Soviet Bloc nor the Nasser-dominated Arab League.

BRITAIN, ADEN AND THE GULF

After the Suez war Britain's Middle Eastern presence was reduced to Aden and the Gulf. Protection of oil interests was seen as the first concern, followed by treaty obligations. The 1957 British Defence White Paper advocated the need for a new approach, especially because earlier plans had depended on expenditure that was by 1957 well beyond the capacity of the country to meet.[18] It recognised that the Communist threat had changed and that most of Britain's obligations would be fulfilled within NATO and CENTO, but emphasis was laid on the importance of Aden and East Africa. A carrier group was to be stationed in the Indian Ocean, supported by a United Kingdom reserve which could be transported by air when necessary. In April 1959 the Arabia Peninsula command was built up, and in October a unified command was created at Aden.

The 1962 White Paper, *The Next Five Years*, went on to define British policy still further, although the Kuwaiti expedition (see below, pp. 138–9) had shown how difficult this kind of policy was to carry out.[19]

Peace and stability in the oil-producing states of Arabia and the Persian Gulf are vital for the Western world. We are, and still remain responsible for military assistance to those States in the area to which we are bound by treaty or which are otherwise under our protection. ... For further possible operations in the Gulf we have relied on Aden as a base and on reinforcing from Kenya. Henceforward we plan to keep land forces permanently stationed in Aden and the Gulf and to reinforce them rapidly in emergency not only by air, but also by means of an amphibious joint service task force East of Suez capable of putting ashore in the threatened areas land forces, and their heavy equipment, and of providing air and communications support.[20]

Meanwhile within Aden itself the growth of nationalism was beginning to set new problems for the British administrators. Gradual concessions to demands for representation were being made. A Legislative Council was created in 1947, twelve of whose members were nominated by the Governor. In 1955 the Council was enlarged slightly, and allowed to have four elected members. Appeals for a more speedy advance to self-government were made to Lord

Lloyd, the Under-Secretary of State for the Colonies, in May 1956, when he visited the Colony. Assuring them that self-government would come eventually, he said: 'Her Majesty's Government wish to make it clear that the importance of Aden both strategically and economically within the Commonwealth is such that they cannot foresee the possibility of any fundamental relaxation of their responsibilities for the Colony.'[21] Further concessions were granted in 1958 when the official majority predominance in the Legislative Council was abolished, and Arabic was permitted as an alternative language to English. The increasing power of the Trade Unions provided an important element in the growth of nationalist demands in Aden.

In the 1950s talks began on a suggested federation of the States of the Protectorate. These were a group of small emirates which had gradually been brought under the nominal protection of the British Government. Mr (later Sir Kennedy) Trevaskis put forward the initial scheme, which promised in the first place two separate federations, one for the Western Protectorate and one for the Eastern. The High Commissioner of the area was to be the Governor of Aden. The scheme met opposition from the first. As one nationalist said later; 'In Aden we are opposed to Yemen because it is feudal, but there is only one Imam there. There will be 26 Imams in the Federation.'[22] By 1956 Britain had reduced its suggestion to an offer to help the States 'to seek some form of close association with each other for mutual assistance and support', which the 'rulers and peoples of these states are entirely free to negotiate among themselves'.[23]

British relations with Kuwait were happier. The development of the oil industry in the State brought great prosperity. By 1960 Kuwait was supplying Britain with 37.6 per cent of her total crude oil import, and what was of great importance, the Kuwait Oil Company dealt in sterling. Britain abandoned her control over Kuwaiti foreign

policy in January 1961, and on 19 June complete independence was granted. Britain's relationship with the State
was summarised by the British Political Resident in the
Persian Gulf in a letter to the ruler of Kuwait: 'The relations
between the two countries shall continue to be governed by
a spirit of close friendship', and 'when appropriate the
two Governments shall consult together on matters which
concern them both'.[24] The friendship was soon put to the
test when Kassem laid claim to the State, and declared
that it was an 'integral part' of Iraq. The Royal Navy
commando carrier, H.M.S. *Bulwark*, was told to stand by.
On 30 June the Ruler asked for British help, and troops
were landed from the carrier. The danger from Iraq was
averted, but criticism of the action was made in several
quarters. Some felt that it was a United Nations matter.
Others in Britain felt that it proved the inadequacy of the
Government's new defence policy which thrust unacclima-
tised troops into the difficult conditions of the Gulf.

It has often been argued that Kuwait provided a good
pattern for the granting of independence in the Gulf and
southern Arabia, and one that might be followed in Aden
and elsewhere. The difference between Kuwait and the
other States is an economic one. Kuwait's great wealth
made her immediately viable as an independent State.
Even Aden itself has not such a secure economy, while the
emirates of the Protectorate and the Sheikhdoms of the
Gulf are underdeveloped and without resources.

On 11 February 1959 the Western States of the Protectorate signed a treaty of federation. Britain promised
protection and financial and military aid. Each State was
to elect six members for the Federal Council and it, in its
turn, would elect a Supreme Council which would have
legislative powers. In January 1963 Britain linked the colony
of Aden with the Federation. The reason for promoting the
idea of federation at all was, as Sir Charles Johnston the
Governor said, to prevent the disruption of the area by

Yemeni nationalists.[25] Economically the addition of Aden
would help the region to become a workable entity, but
nationalism is rarely moved by economic arguments, and
the port disliked being linked with the Protectorate. The
Eastern Protectorate, a barren area twice as large as the
Western region, did not commit itself to the Foundation.

The problems of Aden were complicated by the Yemeni
war. In September 1962 civil war broke out in the country,
and Egyptian troops were sent in by Nasser to help the
revolutionary government.[26] Egyptian propaganda affected
political groups in the Colony and the Protectorate. The
Egyptian-backed Front for the Liberation of South Yemen
(FLOSY) and the National Liberation Front (NLF) have
contributed a great share to the growth of violence in Aden.
The United Nations Colonial Committee passed a resolution in June 1966, declaring that the Federal Government
was unrepresentative; nevertheless it suggested sending a
mission out to the Colony to investigate the situation before
independence was granted in January 1968. A three-man
mission arrived in Aden in April 1967, but was unable to
make contact with the nationalist groups, and it left after
a few days with its work uncompleted. As violence mounted
in the spring and summer of 1967 the whole question of
Britain's survival in the port and the necessity of keeping
a base was debated.[27] In May Sir Humphrey Trevelyan, a
diplomat experienced in Arab affairs and well known as a
realistic negotiator, was called out of retirement to become
High Commissioner. After several months of extreme
terrorism and virtual loss of control by the British, he
announced the recognition of 'the nationalist forces as
representatives of the people'.[28] Many questions remain to
be resolved; the struggle for power between the nationalist
groups, the withdrawal of the British, and the future of the
small States of the Protectorate. 'From the British point of
view a rather more representative group than the former
federal government has materialised just in time for the

flag-hauling ceremony. And since South Arabia is not a country Britain can leave without humiliation of one sort or another, maybe the sooner the flag comes down the better.'[29]

FRANCE AND INDEPENDENT NORTH AFRICA

De Gaulle's attitude to North Africa was conditioned by the Algerian problem which he was pledged to solve when he came to power. It led in some cases to tactless treatment of the two other powers who had just gained their independence, but whose new régimes were still sympathetic to France. Both Bourguiba of Tunisia and Mohammed V of Morocco offered their mediation in the Algerian negotiations, but their offers were rejected by France. The bombing of the Tunisian border village of Sakiet Sidi Youssef by French aeroplanes, killing as it did seventy-five people and wounding eighty-nine others, was an unnecessary incident which strained relations between France and Tunisia, and roused universal criticism at a time when France needed all the moral support she could get. Bourguiba began negotiations for the removal of the remaining 15,000 French troops from his country, and asked that the future of the French naval and air base at Bizerta should be discussed. Morocco, preoccupied at the time with disputes on her southern frontier with Mauritania, also asked for the evacuation of French troops. In June 1958 de Gaulle conceded these demands although the question of Bizerta remained.

The settlement arrived at in the second Evian talks left the French President free to return to the problems of Europe which he preferred, but he considered the granting of aid to countries which had formerly been part of the French Empire an essential part of the re-building of the French image.[30] The French role in both Tunisia and Morocco remained enormous.[31] Before the 1961 Bizerta crisis France financed the major part of the Tunisian educational system; she paid for nearly half the cost of

French teachers serving in the country, and financed
Tunisians receiving special training in France. Similarly,
in Morocco, France provided teachers and doctors, and
encouraged Moroccans to study in France. French investment was not withdrawn from the countries, and France
continued to receive the greater part of their exports. The
colons who remained were assimilated into the new States,
happily in Tunisia and with a greater degree of restraint in
Morocco.[32] The Government of Tunisia under the moderate
Habib Bourguiba remained pro-Western, and has continued
to hold a middle course between the politics of the Arab
League and those of the West. In Morocco Ahmed Balafrej, the Foreign Minister, always an admirer of French
culture, advocated a blending of the two civilisations,
Islamic and French.

Algeria's bitter struggle for independence inevitably left
deeper scars on her people. The FLN had from the first
rejected assimilation. Malek Haddad, speaking in Beirut in
1961, blamed France for Algeria's situation as 'the most
perfidious case of depersonalisation in history'.[33] In the
years after the Second World War an important group of
Algerian intellectuals had protested against French policy
and culture, making their protest, ironically enough, in
French. Frantz Fanon's *The Wretched of the Earth* (*Les
damnés de la terre*), was one of the most famous anti-colonial
books produced by the revolution.[34] The first generation of
Algerian politicians, Ferhat Abbas, Ben Bella, and others,
like the early intellectuals, appeared to the rising group of
Arabic speakers as half Frenchmen. The overthrow of
Ahmed Ben Bella by Colonel Houari Boumedienne in
June 1965 was the second stage in the revolution begun by
the war against France.

The search for a new identity affected all the North
African countries in varying degrees; all three still felt on a
balance between the West and the Arab world. On 1 October
1958 both Tunisia and Morocco joined the Arab League.

Tunisia's relationship with it was brief and unhappy. Personal hostility existed between the two Presidents Bourguiba and Nasser, Bourguiba alleging that the Egyptian leader was supporting his political rival, Salah ben Youssef, and intended to overthrow him. Morocco was more satisfied with the aims of the Arab League. In September 1959 it met under the auspices of Mohammed V in Casablanca, and the King put forward a plan 'for a conference of heads of Arab states to examine the new responsibilities of the League and decide ways of solving the problems, internal and external, facing the Arab world'.[35] A year later, in August 1960, Morocco obtained the support of the League for her claim to Mauritania. Tunisia on this occasion disagreed with Moroccan demands, thus demonstrating the tensions which existed among the independent states of the Maghrib.

On 25 January 1960, Bourguiba again raised the question of Bizerta with France.[36] His motives were obscure. It may have been, as he said later, because of 'a vestige of colonism which was hindering our relations with France'. It was also the anniversary of the bombing of Sakiet and he may have felt the need to show his independence of France. De Gaulle called his bluff and said France would defend Bizerta if necessary. In the summer of 1961 the matter was referred to the Security Council, which recorded a vote in favour of Tunisia. Moderation of both the French and Tunisian sides after the affair quickly restored good relations between the two countries. The base was finally evacuated in October 1963.

General de Gaulle's restoration of French prestige and his defiance of the United States did much more to rebuild France's reputation in North Africa and the Arab world than any programme of aid could do. Indeed there were indications in the Jeanneney Report of 1964 that this programme was to be cut progressively, and complete reliance put on France's cultural influence. But tensions still remained.

France's ambitions in the Sahara touch one of Algeria's tender spots, and Colonel Boumedienne's régime is less likely to compromise than the negotiators of Evian. French relations with Morocco were strained by the Ben Barka affair. Whether the capture of the Moroccan left-wing leader and his assumed murder in Paris 1965 was 'une affaire simple qui se passe entre coquins', as M. Bourges, the French Head of Information, declared, or a political plot in which a number of distinguished French politicians were involved, has not yet become clear even after two trials, nor have the complicated motives behind the action been explained.[37] Whatever the truth of the matter, it showed that Paris was still keeping a careful watch on North African politics.

EGYPT AND ISRAEL IN THE SIXTIES

Nasser's honeymoon period with the Arabs did not last long into the sixties. In September 1961 a Syrian coup brought to power a new régime which broke the ties with Egypt; the Ba'ath Party had realised that their socialism was very different from Nasser's. The Egyptian leader admitted that the union had never been an easy one. 'During the past three and a half years, we faced many difficulties in Syria. We faced endless troubles. Almost three-quarters of my time was spent in solving Syria's problems and over-coming its difficulties and hardships.'[38] He turned to home affairs again and issued a National Charter in May 1962 to rebuild Egypt, but here economic difficulties were overwhelming.

The United States which had supported Egypt with food and financial aid gradually lost interest in this particular venture; the change from the Kennedy administration to the Johnson, and the intensification of the Vietnamese war, accounted for the revision of America's policy.[39] Egypt's commitments in the Yemeni war from 1962 onwards grew rapidly, and men and money were thrown away in hopeless guerrilla warfare that did not even bring Nasser prestige in the Arab world, and certainly convinced the West of his political irresponsibility. In the course of 1965 and 1966 he fostered anti-American propaganda, snubbed British diplomats because of British Aden and Rhodesian policies, and encouraged anti-Israeli feeling, always near the surface, in an attempt to restore his position in the Arab world.

Meanwhile Israel was also suffering from internal difficulties. Georges Friedmann, in a perceptive and challenging book, *The End of the Jewish People?*, has discussed many of the problems.[40] The original pioneers were giving way to a younger, more affluent Israeli-born generation, whose roots were completely in the Middle East, and who wanted the assurance of a settled future. In political terms the dilemma has been clear in the disputes between the Prime Minister, the moderate Levi Eshkol, and the dynamic Moshe Dayan. The latter felt bitterly that the military gains of the 1956 Suez War had been thrown away by the politicians. His experience both as Minister of Agriculture in the Eshkol government, and as Minister of Defence in the 1967 war, convinced him that he must hold out for Arab recognition of Israel.

THE JORDAN WATERS DISPUTE

The day-to-day aggravation of Arab-Israeli relations was illustrated by their negotiations over the Jordan waters. Shortage of water has been a major factor in the slowness of economic development in the Middle East. The river Jordan, although its flow is not regular and passes through the salt Lake Tiberias, provided one of the few opportunities for large-scale irrigation which would benefit both Israel and Jordan. In 1954 President Eisenhower sent a special representative, Mr Eric Johnston, to the Middle East to discuss the plans presented by the Arabs and Israelis, and to put forward his own solution.[41] The Johnston plan suggested joint exploitation which would give 60 per cent of the annual flow to Jordan and 40 per cent to Israel. It foundered on the political quarrels of 1955–6. The Israelis were loath to depend on sharing this valuable asset with hostile Arabs; the Arabs did not want the Israelis to pump water away from the Jordan basin, nor did they like the idea of a fertile and Israeli-settled Negev.

Population pressure brought the issue forward again in the 1960s, and each side began its own scheme.[42] Israel started pumping water out of Lake Tiberias, and after initial difficulties, had to introduce a water-purifying plant. In 1961 the Jordanians put a pre-war plan into operation. They diverted part of the flow of the tributary river Yarmuk through the East Ghor Canal to irrigate their land. But political trammels still encumbered the projects. The Arabs, Lebanese and Syrians as well as the Jordanians, evolved a scheme to divert the headwaters of the Jordan by altering the courses of the Baniyas and Hasbaya rivers, which would stop the flow of fresh water into Lake Tiberias and damage Israeli agriculture by increasing the salinity.

THE 1967 ARAB-ISRAELI WAR

The build-up of arms and the brinkmanship practised by both sides led to a situation in June 1967 which resulted in war.* Nasser closed the Gulf of Aqaba to Israeli shipping, ordered the UN force to leave Sinai, and both sides mobilised. On 5 June war broke out – it is still not clear who fired the first shot – and by the end of the week Israel had defeated the Arabs decisively on all fronts, Egyptian, Syrian and Jordanian.[43] The whole of the city of Jerusalem and the west bank of the Jordan were in Israeli hands, and

---

* The Western reporting of the events was, as in the earlier Suez war, biased in favour of the Israelis because information was more easily obtainable from this source.

Foreign Office,
November 2nd, 1917.

ar Lord Rothschild,

I have much pleasure in conveying to you, on
alf of His Majesty's Government, the following
claration of sympathy with Jewish Zionist aspirations
ich has been submitted to, and approved by, the Cabinet.

"His Majesty's Government view with favour the
establishment in Palestine of a national home for the
Jewish people, and will use their best endeavours to
facilitate the achievement of this object, it being
clearly understood that nothing shall be done which
may prejudice the civil and religious rights of
existing non-Jewish communities in Palestine, or the
rights and political status enjoyed by Jews in any
other country".

I should be grateful if you would bring this
claration to the knowledge of the Zionist Federation.

2a. The Mosul Commission, 1925

2b. Amir (later king) Abdullah of Transjordan

2c. General (later Marshal) Lyautey in Morocco

3. Lord Plumer

4*a*. General Gouraud, French administrator

4*b*. The 'Big Inch', the pipe-line from Kirkuk to Banias under construction in 1952

5. Violent opposition
Above: Blowing up of the King David Hotel, July 1946
Below: Plastic bomb explosion in Paris, January 1962

6 *and* 7. Characters in Suez drama

Opposite, above: M. Pineau and Sir
   Anthony Eden
Opposite, below: Mr John Foster Dulles
Above left: M. Mollet, French Prime
   Minister
Above right: Mr David Ben Gurion
Right: President Nasser

8. Change in North Africa

Above: M. Habib Bourguiba
Below: President de Gaulle – 'Je vous ai compris'

the east bank of the Suez Canal. Thousands of Arab refugees had left their homes to create a new international problem. Britain and the United States had attempted to avert open warfare by diplomacy, and the United States sent their Sixth Fleet to stand by in the Eastern Mediterranean. Britain was accused by the Arabs of helping the Israelis, the oil supply from the Middle East was disrupted, but neither she nor the United States could have intervened. Russia, in spite of supplying Egypt with arms, appears to have urged moderation on her protegée, and both the Russians and President Tito of Yugoslavia have discussed future policy in the Middle East with the Arabs since the fighting ceased.

The problems remain. If no settlement is reached, the danger is that the next Suez war may be a nuclear one, and the difficulties in the way of a settlement are enormous. The Arabs, humiliated by this second Israeli victory in just over ten years, have to find a peace that can be made with honour. Nasser has agreed to negotiate with Saudi Arabia about the withdrawal of Egyptian troops from Yemen, and at the Arab summit meeting in Khartoum the participants agreed to allow oil to flow again to the West. But the Suez Canal is still closed at the time of writing and no Arab has suggested recognition of Israel. In Israel fierce arguments rage between the supporters of the 'soft line' of Levi Eshkol and the 'hard line' of Moshe Dayan. It will be difficult for Israel to be charitable in victory.

The role of third parties in this situation is not yet clear. The United Nations received a blow by the removal of the peace-keeping force. Neither the advances of the United States nor of Russia seem welcome to either party in the dispute. Of the former imperial powers in the Middle East, France still has some standing because of de Gaulle's anti-American policy, but Britain will have little part to play until her presence is completely removed from the area by withdrawal from Aden.

W.B.F.

NOTES ON CHAPTER 8

1. H. G. Nicholas, 'Progress at the United Nations', in A. Moncrieff (ed.), *Suez Ten Years After* (London, 1967), pp. 127–34.
2. Ibid. p. 131.
3. Sir Anthony Eden, *Full Circle* (London, 1960), p. 557.
4. Paul Bareau and C. M. Woodhouse in Moncrieff, op. cit. pp. 24–9, and Hugh Thomas, *The Suez Affair* (London, 1967), pp. 145–6.
5. Hugh Thomas, op. cit. p. 147.
6. Robert Murphy, *Diplomat among Warriors* (London, 1964), pp. 463–3. Mr Macmillan's autobiography has not yet reached this period of his career.
7. Anthony Nutting, *No End of a Lesson: the Story of Suez* (London, 1967) explains why one junior Minister resigned on the issue.
8. John Erickson, in Moncrieff, op. cit. pp. 21–4.
9. The votes on the various questions asked in the opinion polls are discussed in Moncrieff, op. cit. pp. 19–20.
10. Thomas, op. cit. p. 148.
11. Moshe Dayan, *Diary of the Sinai Campaign* (London, 1965), p. 207.
12. For the constitution and policy of the Ba'ath Party see Sylvia Haim (ed.), *Arab Nationalism: An Anthology* (Berkeley and Los Angeles, 1964), pp. 233–49.
13. See J. Eayrs (ed.), *The Commonwealth and Suez; a Documentary Survey* (Oxford, 1964).
14. Robert Rhodes James, 'Political Echoes', in Moncrieff, op. cit. p. 115.
15. Monroe, p. 208.
16. Pierre Rondot, 'July Days', in *Changing Patterns of the Middle East 1919–1958* (London, 1961), pp. 13–22.
17. Malcolm Kerr, 'Coming to terms with Nasser', in *International Affairs* (January, 1967), pp. 73–6.
18. Defence, outline of future policy, Cmd. 124 (London, April 1957) clause 2.
19. *Statement on Defence; the next five years, February, 1962* (London, 1962).
20. Ibid. clause 17.
21. Gillian King, *Imperial Outpost – Aden* (London, 1964), p. 48.
22. Ibid. p. 68.
23. Ibid. p. 59.

24. R.I.I.A. Documents on International Affairs, 1961 (London, 1965), p. 771.
25. Sir Charles Johnston, *The View from Steamer Point: Being an Account of Three Years in Aden* (London, 1964), p. 195.
26. David Holden, *Farewell to Arabia* (London, 1966), pp. 69–115.
27. For the arguments for the British leaving Aden see Elizabeth Monroe, 'British bases in the Middle East; assets or liabilities?', in *International Affairs*, vol. 42 (1966), pp. 24–34.
    For arguments against see J. B. Kelly, 'The future in Arabia', in the same, pp. 619–40.
28. *The Times*, 6 Sept. 1967.
29. *The Economist*, 9 Sept. 1967, p. 875.
30. Alfred Grosser, 'General de Gaulle and the foreign policy of the Fifth Republic', in *International Affairs*, vol. 39, 1963.
31. David C. Gordon, *North Africa's French Legacy, 1954–1962* (Cambridge, Mass., 1962), pp. 16–22.
32. Ibid., pp. 20–1.
33. Ibid. p. 36.
34. Published by Penguin Books in 1967.
35. R.I.I.A. Survey of International Affairs, 1959–60 (London, 1964), pp. 350–1.
36. Ibid. p. 355.
37. Daniel Sarne, *L'Affaire Ben Barka* (Paris, 1966).
38. Speech of 29 September, quoted in Peter Mansfield, *Nasser's Egypt* (London, 1965), p. 63.
39. Malcolm Kerr, op. cit. pp. 77–84.
40. Georges Friedmann, *The End of the Jewish People?* (English edition, London, 1967).
41. Georgiana G. Stevens, *Jordan River Partition* (Stanford, 1965), pp. 17–32.
42. Elizabeth Monroe, in *The Times*, 11 May, 1965.
43. Randolph S. and Winston S. Churchill, *The Six Day War* (London, 1967).

Postscript
Britain and France in the Middle East and North Africa

THE fiftieth anniversary of the Balfour Declaration occurred in November 1967. Its publication in 1917 had passed with little comment in Britain, and Balfour went to his grave thinking it 'the most worthwhile thing to which he had ever set his hand'.[1] It was ironic that the same month should see the premature withdrawal of British troops from Aden with no hope of leaving a stable government behind.

In the years before the First World War the aims of British policy in the Middle East were reasonably straightforward. The defence of India and its trade routes was of overwhelming importance, and the protection of the Suez Canal had a high priority in the decisions taken. The strength of the forces in India and of the navy enabled the British to take on paternal obligations for the security of the Trucial Sheikhdoms, and the protection of the sea lanes from piracy. Aden was built up as a base and flourished in its new expansion. Egypt, where control was gradually and unwillingly assumed by the British, was brought into closer contact by the First World War itself. This piecemeal acquisition of 'empire' developed in response to the needs of the moment, and was not planned by Whitehall or Delhi.

The collapse of the Ottoman Empire brought with it new problems to confront the statesmen of the West, who were already exhausted by the unprecedented strain of a world war. It was not surprising that mistakes were made.

Alliances were needed and promises were given. The quixotic gesture to the Zionists was a mixture of idealism, the desire to win allies after the collapse of Tsarist Russia, and the need to protect the Suez Canal. The effect of the Declaration was underestimated, as was the future of Arab nationalism as a driving force in the Middle East. The divisions and political inexperience of the Arab leaders put them at a disadvantage in dealing with the Peace-makers. 'At the time, their loyalties were to tribe, district and township; in the Arabian peninsula, Ibn Saud and the Sharif of Mecca were on bad terms: farther north, minorities of all kinds – Druses, Christian communities Kurds and others – gave their allegiance to leading families; there was no cadre of army officers from which a Kemal or a Reza Khan might spring; towns were nervous of bedouin ascendancy; the desert mistrusted the town.'[2] The Western powers were confident that Mandatory tutelage in Palestine and Syria offered the best hope for the prosperity of the area. Their presence gave the nationalists, there as else-where, a focus for their protest which ignored the benefits received from the West, and on many occasions even their own economic interest.

The inter-war period also saw the birth and growth of the oil industry. It was a matter of chance that the oilfields of Iran lay next to the British sphere of influence, and that Kirkuk, Basra, Kuwait, Qatar and Abu Dhabi lay on the route to India, but Britain was able to profit from the discoveries. In 1948, a year after India had gained her independence, the Marshall Aid Plan created a greater demand for Middle Eastern oil, and a new incentive to safeguard sea and land routes from the area. The Middle Eastern countries were able to take advantage of the sellers' market they enjoyed from the 1940s to the post-1956-Suez-war period, and although the British Government rarely intervened to protect its interests, identifica-tion between company and government was complete in the Arab and Persian mind. Thus the industry attracted 'a whole gamut of local grievances, including some that had nothing to do with oil – chagrin about social inequality, resentment at Western power, anger at the indignity of watching the one great national resource used for the profit of foreigners.'[3]

One of the lessons of the 1956 Suez war was, however, that Europe might look for oil elsewhere, or even develop alternative sources of energy, like natural gas. The exploitation of oil in North Africa and Nigeria (Biafra) lessened dependence on Middle Eastern oil; in 1966 only 47.9 per cent of Britain's requirements was met by the Middle Eastern countries.[4] It has been estimated that Britain could survive the denial of two of these sources without hardship. This change in demand was reflected by the anxiety of the oil-producing states at the disruption of their exports by the Arab-Israeli War of 1967, and by the closing of the Suez Canal.

The Second World War and its aftermath drew attention to Britain's weakness, but gave her no opportunity to break away from traditional and newly assumed responsibilities in the Middle East. Declining authority and continual economic crisis left her powerless to support her economic interests, or her old friends. Ties with the Hashemite rulers were gradually broken, by the death of Feisal in the 1958 Iraqi *coup d'état*, and the *rapprochement* between Hussein of Jordan and Nasser before the 1967 Arab-Israeli war. The treaties of friendship with the Trucial Sheikhdoms can probably no longer be observed. Withdrawal from Palestine, Egypt and Aden was only achieved with humiliation. It was easy for the Arab world to make political capital out of the British position.

France's commitments in North Africa were the result of her traditional interests in the Mediterranean reinterpreted in terms of the nineteenth century. Her Mediterranean coastline had been vulnerable in the

Middle Ages, and if her preoccupations in Europe tended to obscure her southern interests these interests nevertheless remained a consistent element in policy. Her trading and cultural links with the eastern Mediterranean were re-emphasised as a result of Napoleon's expedition to Egypt, and the French revolutionary ideas which he took with him penetrated the fastnesses of Islam and laid it open to Western influence. Side by side with this, French Catholic missions spread in the Levant, and French investment developed the Levant commercially and strengthened the ties with France.

The opening of the Suez Canal made the Mediterranean once more a central point of European attention instead of the backwater it had been since the sixteenth century. European rivalries, particularly those between Britain and France, turned France's attention to her security and interests in the south. The invasions in North Africa were undertaken to meet the challenges of the day, but once a foothold had been gained it seemed impossible not to extend operations over the intractable hinterland which had defeated its Turkish overlords. In Algeria, in particular, occupation was a hard struggle which was resisted for over fifty years by the indigenous population. By the time it was accomplished the idea of colonial territories was becoming acceptable, and even seemed necessary for France's position as a European power of the first rank.

By the turn of the century, too, a *colon* population had been built up with its own special demands on the mother country, and with its powerful voice in policy towards North Africa. Virtually untroubled by the events of the First World War, the French position was strengthened by their administrative and educational programme. The natural leaders of any opposition to French rule were disarmed by their attachment to French culture, and it was a long time before they had confidence in the identity of their own countries. Isolated from the main Arab nationalist movement, North African Arabs found themselves in an ambiguous position between Europe and the Middle East, which they still have not resolved.

The dramatic defeat of France in the Second World War made her decline as a colonial power more obvious than that of Britain. Expelled from Lebanon and Syria, she turned to meet organised opposition in North Africa. The overthrow of the Fourth Republic and the emergence of de Gaulle gave the appearance of a complete break with the past which enabled France to develop new relationships with her former possessions, in a way which has been completely denied to Britain. For both the Middle East and North Africa, de Gaulle represents the challenge to the strength of the United States which they themselves would like to make.

Many problems remain in the Middle East and North Africa, but successive crises, and particularly the Suez war of 1956, showed that active intervention by Britain and France was no longer an acceptable path to their solution. Now that the fear of great powers rushing in to fill the vacuum in the area has diminished, the only course for the former imperialist powers seems to be to do nothing, and to be seen to do nothing. It may then be that the West and the Middle East can meet on equal terms in the future.

NOTES TO POSTSCRIPT

1. Elizabeth Monroe, 'How Balfour persuaded the Cabinet', in *The Times*, 2 November 1967.
2. Monroe, p. 212–13.
3. Monroe, p. 114.
4. *The Times*, 14 November 1967.

Appendix

NOTE ON THE HISTORIOGRAPHY
OF SUEZ AND THE ISSUE OF
COLLUSION

THE historiography of Suez is as complex as the events themselves. The last few years have seen the appearance of a number of books on the events of the summer of 1956 (see Bibliography). Michel Bar-Zohar's two contributions to the study of the problem, *Suez Ultra Secret*, and *Ben Gourion, prophète armé*, are very useful. He had access to Ben Gurion's papers, and has made good use of them for Franco-Israeli relations and the steps leading to the November invasion. Henri Azeau's *Le Piège de Suez* is the most detailed account of the campaign; its viewpoint is anti-British. Azeau interviewed French ministers involved in the affair, and M. Pineau added comments of his own in a BBC programme on Suez in the summer of 1966. His remarks on this occasion were summed up by Elizabeth Monroe in the *Observer*, on 24 July 1966, and have subsequently been published in the BBC book, *Suez Ten Years After*.

Herman Finer wrote a bitter attack on Dulles in *Dulles Over Suez*, but there is a great deal of information in the book. The memoirs of President Eisenhower, volume 2, *Waging Peace*, and Robert Murphy, *Diplomat Among Warriors*, provide further evidence on American policy. Moshe Dayan has published his *Diary of the Sinai Campaign*. President Nasser gave an interview to the BBC which is printed in *Suez Ten Years After*, but otherwise there are no Arab accounts of the events.

The English point of view is still badly represented. Sir Anthony Eden's volume of memoirs, *Full Circle*, is evasive. Anthony Nutting's, *No End of a Lesson: the Story of Suez* traces the effect of Eden's illness on events, and is an apologia for Nutting's own decision to resign. The chief contributions come from Terence Robertson and Hugh Thomas. The former, a Canadian, had the advice of Lester Pearson, Canadian Minister for External Affairs in 1956, for his *Crisis: the Inside Story of the Suez Conspiracy*. Hugh Thomas's *The Suez Affair* summarises the evidence concisely, and will probably be the standard version for some years to come. But both these books suffer from the defect of relying so much on unsupported conversations. Reminiscences unbacked by documentary evidence are notoriously unreliable. More memoirs are promised and these will fill in other gaps. The documents will not be available for many years; many have been destroyed and much negotiation took place on the telephone. Probably we shall never touch the bottom of the events of 1956.

THE ISSUE OF COLLUSION

'We must wait. If there was collusion, the motives of the men who practised it were so various that, sooner or later, they are bound to start giving one another away.' The issue that provoked this remark by Hugh Gaitskell, the Leader of the Opposition, as early as 1956, was the doubt that the Eden government's version of the Suez invasion was the true one. Eden maintained that Britain only intervened to stop the Israeli-Egyptian war. The earlier alliances of France and Israel, and of France and Britain, although kept secret for obvious reasons of diplomacy, were not at issue. The question of deceit in the methods of diplomacy, which is what the charge of collusion implies, centred round the British-Israeli negotiations.

The British government had a great deal to lose by the disclosure of its close co-operation with Israel. In the first place the position Britain held in the Arab world, and in 1956 it was still a considerable position, would be destroyed. Secondly, if the United States knew the extent of the plans to overthrow Nasser, she would intervene to stop the attempt. Lastly Eden risked provoking divisions in both the Cabinet and the country if the deliberate nature of the aggression were known.

Questioned in the House of Commons by Gaitskell on 31 October 1956, before the Anglo-French attack, Selwyn Lloyd denied the rumours of collusion:

It is quite wrong to state that Israel was incited to this action by Her Majesty's Government. There was no prior agreement between us about it. It is, of course, true that the Israeli mobilisation gave some advance warning, and we urged restraint upon the Israeli Government and, in particular, drew attention to the serious consequences of any attack on Jordan.

Later the questioners probed the theory that there was at least foreknowledge of the Israeli attack, and Anthony Eden spoke about this suggestion in the Commons on 20 December 1956:

We have been accused of being, ever since the Israeli attack on Egypt, and indeed long before that, in collusion with the Israelis. My Rt. Hon. and Learned Friend the Foreign Secretary emphatically denied that charge on 31st October. Since then, it seems that the charge has been altered and Her Majesty's Government have been asked to prove that they had no foreknowledge of the Israeli attack.
There were certainly a number of indications of an increasingly dangerous situation, particularly, as we thought, between Israel and Jordan. We warned the Israeli Government of the consequences of an attack on Jordan, and we gave a number of warnings, including the general warning to which my Rt. Hon. Learned Friend referred. But to say – and this is what I want to repeat to the House – that Her Majesty's Government were engaged in some dishonourable conspiracy is completely untrue, and I most emphatically deny it.' [Again at the end of the debate he repeated] 'I want to say this on the question of foreknowledge, and to say it quite bluntly to the House, that there was not foreknowledge that Israel would attack.'

Although the rumours continued, the matter rested there until 1964 when a number of books were produced on the Suez war. Azeau, Bar-Zohar and Finer interviewed the French ministers concerned in the affair who, unlike their British colleagues, had nothing to hide, and obtained information about secret negotiations between Britain, France and Israel in Paris in mid-October 1956. Two years later, Christian Pineau, the French Foreign Minister at the time of Suez, in a BBC interview, revealed that a tripartite treaty had been signed at Sèvres on 23–24 October. Anthony Nutting does not mention a treaty in his book, but refers to the Paris consultations. Anthony Eden and Selwyn Lloyd have added nothing to their earlier statements, but Christian Pineau has said: 'And I think maybe after ten years it would be possible to say more, and if one day my English friends of this period accept to say all the truths about this question, I should agree.'*

* *Suez Ten Years After*, p. 95.

Chronological Table

1830   French Conquest of Algeria.

1869   Suez Canal opened.

1881   French protectorate over Tunisia.

1882   British occupation of Egypt.

1907   French protectorate over Morocco.

1914
9 September	Turkish abolition of Capitulations.
30 October	Turkey declares war against Entente.
18 December	British Protectorate over Egypt.

1915
4 March	First tripartite partition of Middle East.
April	de Bunsen Committee in London discusses alternative plans for disposal of Ottoman empire.
26 April	Treaty of London.
14 July	Hussein–McMahon correspondence began (continued until 30 January 1916. Not published officially until 1939).

1916
May	Sykes–Picot agreement.
April	Fall of Kut.
10 June	Arab revolt begins.

1917
11 March	Baghdad taken.
15–21 April	Treaty of St-Jean-de-Maurienne.
2 November	Balfour declaration.
9 December	Jerusalem taken.

1918
8 January	President Wilson's Fourteen Points.
1 October	Damascus taken.

1918   30 October   Allied armistice with Turkey at Mudros.

8 November   Anglo-French declaration to Arabs.

1919   Peace conference at Versailles.

29 January   Emir Feisal asks for independence for Arabs.

June–July   King–Crane commission. (Report not published until 1922.)

Riots in Egypt.

1920   18–25 April   San Remo conference.

25 July   French evict King Feisal from Damascus.

10 August   Treaty of Sèvres.

December   Milner report published.

Destour party founded in Tunisia.

1921   12 March   Cairo conference.

23 August   King Feisal crowned in Baghdad.

1922   28 February   Egyptian independence recognised.

16 September   Transjordan separated from Palestine.

10 October   Anglo-Iraqi treaty.

1923   May   Transjordan independent with British protection.

29 October   Turkey declared Republic.

1924   30 October   King Hussein evicted from Mecca by Ibn Saud.

19 November   Murder of Sir Lee Stack.

1925   24 July   Syrian revolt against French.

12 October   Lyautey leaves Morocco.

16 December   Iraq given vilayet of Mosul.

1926   8 January   Ibn Saud unites Hejaz and Nejd.

26 May   Rising of Abd el-Krim in Moroccan Rif.

1927　20 May　　　Jiddah treaty between Great Britain and Ibn Saud.

　　　25 October　　Oil found at Kirkuk in Iraq.

　　　18 November　Mohammed V succeeds to Moroccan throne.

1928　20 February　Anglo-Transjordanian agreement.

　　　24 September　Wailing Wall incident in Jerusalem.

1929　August　　　Disturbances in Palestine.

1930　May　　　　Centenary commemoration in Algeria.

　　　22 May　　　Constitution in Syria.

　　　30 June　　　Anglo-Iraqi treaty.

1933　29 April　　Revised agreement between Persia and Anglo-Persian Oil Company.

1936　April　　　Beginning of Arab revolt in Palestine.

　　　26 August　　Anglo-Egyptian treaty.

1937　24 January　Franco-Turkish agreement over Alexandretta.

　　　7 July　　　Peel report published.

1941　29 May　　　Eden's Mansion House speech.

　　　8 June　　　Allied forces enter Syria and Lebanon.

　　　June–July　　Syrian disturbances.

　　　28 September　Independence of Syria.

　　　26 November　Independence of Lebanon.

1942　11 May　　　Zionist Biltmore programme announced in New York.

　　　November　　Anglo-American invasion of North Africa.

1943　12 February　'Manifesto of the Algerian People.'

　　　3 June　　　Catroux Governor of Algeria.

　　　August–September National government in Syria and Lebanon.

　　　November　　Crisis in Lebanon.

　　　December　　Creation of Istiqlal party in Morocco.

1944	16 May	Advisory council for Northern Sudan.
	6 November	Assassination of Lord Moyne.
1945	22 March	Arab League formed.
	8 May	Sétif incident.
	13 December	Anglo-French agreement on Middle East policy.
1946	April	Last French troops withdrawn from Syria.
	October	Draft Anglo-Egyptian treaty. (Never ratified.)
1947	12 March	Truman doctrine.
	22 March	Anglo-Jordanian treaty.
	1 September	UNSCOP report published.
	20 September	Algerian statute.
	29 November	UN General Assembly's resolution on Palestine partition.
1948	15 March	Treaty of Alliance between Britain and Transjordan.
	15 May	End of Palestine mandate.
	19 June	Ordinance for Sudan.
1950	28 May–21 June	British, American and French declaration on security in Arab-Israel area.
1951		'Crisis of 1951' in Morocco.
	1 May	Nationalisation of Anglo-Iranian oil company.
	20 September	Turkey admitted to NATO.
	27 October	Egyptian repudiation of 1936 treaty and Sudan Conventions.
1952	July	Egyptian *coup d'état*. Abdication of King Farouk.
	August	Saudis seize Buraimi.
1953	February	Nasser comes to power.

1954 19–20 September   Iran Consortium agreement.
      1 November   Beginning of Algerian revolt.

1955 February   Baghdad Pact formed. (Later called Central Treaty Organisation.)
      9 November   Sir Anthony Eden's Guildhall speech.
      December   Templer mission to Jordan.

1956 February   General Glubb dismissed.
      2 March   Independence of Morocco and Tunisia.
      26 July   Nationalisation of Suez Canal.
      23 October   Arrest of Ben Bella and other Algerian leaders.
      5 November   Franco-British landing in Egypt.
      6 November   Cease-fire.

1957 25 July   Tunisian Republic proclaimed.
      December   Afro-Asian conference in Cairo.

1958 1 February   Syria and Egypt form United Arab Republic.
      8 February   Sakiet Sidi Youssef bombed.
      13 May   Committee of Public Safety in Algeria.
      14 July   Assassination of Feisal II and Nuri es-Said in Iraq. Republic proclaimed.
      16 July   American forces land at Beirut. British parachutists occupy Amman airfield.

1959 1 January   Official beginning of French 5th Republic.

1961 July   Bizerta affair.
      September   Syria secedes from UAR.

1962 9 February   Kassem overthrown in Baghdad.
      March   Evian agreement between France and Algeria.
      July   Algeria independent.

1962	September	Outbreak of Yemeni revolution.
1963	16 January	Federation of Southern Arabia.
	18 November	*Coup d'état* in Iraq.
	10 December	Bomb thrown at Sir Kennedy Trevaskis in Aden.
1964	13–16 January	Arab League discuss Jordan waters dispute.
1965	1 January	Arab Common Market; Jordan, UAR, Syria, Iraq and Kuwait.
	13 June	Ben Bella overthrown by Colonel Houari Boumedienne.
1966	January	Trial of those involved in Ben Barka affair, in Paris.
	Autumn	Disturbances in Aden.
1967	March–April	Increased violence in Aden.
	April	UN Mission to Aden.
	7 April	Mission withdraws with its work uncompleted.
	May	Sir Humphrey Trevelyan High Commissioner in Aden.
	5–9 June	Arab-Israeli war.
	5 September	Sir Humphrey Trevelyan offers to negotiate with nationalists.
	November	British withdrawal from Aden completed.

Bibliography

I. DOCUMENTARY MATERIAL

H.M.S.O. *Documents on British Foreign Policy, 1918–39*, ed. E. L. Woodward and Rohan Butler. First series, vol. iv. Contains plans and discussions on partition of Ottoman Empire.

HUREWITZ, J. C. *Diplomacy in the Near and Middle East* (Princeton, 1956). Vol. ii, 1914–56, is particularly relevant. It has most of the important agreements signed between Britain and the Middle Eastern countries.

The publication of French official documents was delayed by the war. The volumes published contain material on the question of the Straits, and particularly on Franco-Italian ambitions in the Mediterranean.

Ministère des affaires étrangères. Documents diplomatiques français.

(1) 1ère Série, 1932–6, tt. 1 and 2 published (Paris, 1964–6). Covers period Nov. 1932–March 1933.

(2) 2e Série, 1936–9, tt. 1 and 2 (Paris, 1963–4). Period Jan. 1936–July 1936.

Three British Government Command papers are valuable.

Special Commission to Egypt. (The Milner Mission Report). Cmd. 1131 (London, 1921).

Correspondence between Sir Henry McMahon and the Sharif of Mecca. Cmd. 5957 (London, 1939).

Palestine Royal Commission. (The Peel Commission Report). Cmd. 5479 (London, 1937).

The Royal Institute for International Affairs has published documents annually since 1928. The 1956 volume has important documents on the Suez Crisis. (London, 1959).

The following books have documentary material, mostly from the nationalist side, on Algeria and Tunisia.

DEBATTY, A. *Le 13 mai et la Presse* (Paris, 1960).

FAVROD, CHARLES-HENRI. *La Révolution algérienne* (Les documents de Tribune Libre, Paris, 1959).

FAVROD, CHARLES-HENRI. *Le F.L.N. et l'Algérie* (Paris, 1962).

MANDOUZE, ANDRÉ. *La Révolution algérienne par les textes* (Paris, 1961).

ROUS, JEAN. *Tunisie . . . attention!* (Paris, 1952).

Because so little documentary material is yet published, books in the bibliography with documents included are marked with an asterisk.

2. MEMOIRS

General memoirs dealing in some respect with the area:

COOPER, DUFF (LORD NORWICH). *Old Men Forget* (London, 1954). Milner Mission to Egypt, 1919–20.

*DE GAULLE, GENERAL CHARLES. *Mémoires de guerre*, vol. i, *L'appel, 1940–42* (Paris, 1954). Relations between France and Britain in Syria and Lebanon.

EDEN, ANTHONY. *Full Circle* (London, 1960). See also review by Martin Wight in *International Affairs* (1960). Evasive account of author's part in Suez Crisis.

HANKEY, LORD. *The Supreme Command, 1914–18* (2 vols, London, 1961). First World War problems.

Middle East

*BELL, LADY (ed.). *Letters of Gertrude Bell* (vol. ii, London, 1927). British administration in Iraq after First World War. Essay on events by Sir Percy Cox included.

BEGIN, MONACHEM. *The Revolt* (London, 1951). Member of Stern Group in forties.

BELGRAVE, SIR CHARLES. *Personal Column* (London, 1960). Adviser to Sheikh of Bahrain, 1926–57.

BENTWICH, N. and H. *Mandate Memories, 1918–48* (London, 1965).

CATROUX, GENERAL G. *Deux Missions en Moyen Orient 1919–22* (Paris, 1958).

EDMONDS, C. J. *Kurds, Turks and Arabs: Politics, Travel and Research in North-Eastern Iraq, 1919–1925* (London, 1957).

GURION, DAVID BEN. *Rebirth and Destiny of Israel* (first Eng. ed., London, 1959).

JOHNSTON, SIR CHARLES. *The View from Steamer Point: Being an Account of Three Years in Aden* (London, 1964). A tour of duty in Aden, 1960–3.

KIRKBRIDE, SIR ALEC. *A Crackle of Thorns* (London, 1956). British administration in Jordan between the wars.

MEINERTZHAGEN, R. M. *Middle East Diary, 1917–1956* (London, 1959). Member of British Peace Conference staff after First World War.

MURPHY, ROBERT. *Diplomat among Warriors* (London, 1964). US special representative. Important on Suez Crisis.

NASSER, PRESIDENT GAMAL ABDEL. *The Philosophy of the Revolution.* (Cairo, 1954). The Egyptian president's account of his aims.

SAMUEL, VISCOUNT. *Memoirs* (London, 1945). First British High Commissioner in Palestine.

STORRS, SIR RONALD. *Orientations* (London, 1937). Arabia, Cairo and Palestine in First World War and after.

WEIZMANN, CHAIM. *Trial and Error* (London, 1949). Account of the building of Israel.

WILSON, SIR ARNOLD T. *Loyalties: Mesopotamia 1914–1917* (Oxford, 1930), and *Mesopotamia 1917–1920, a clash of loyalties* (Oxford, 1931).

YOUNG, SIR HUBERT. *The Independent Arab* (London, 1933). Secretary of Middle East Department of Colonial Office.

North Africa

ABBAS, FERHAT. *De la colonie vers la province; Le jeune Algérien* (Paris, 1931). *La nuit coloniale* (Paris, 1962). Show development of Algerian leader's ideas.

BIDAULT, GEORGES. *L'Algérie, L'oiseau aux Ailes coupées* (Paris, 1938).

BOURGUIBA, H. *La Tunisie et la France* (Paris, 1954). Tunisian leader's newspaper articles of thirties.

BOYER DE LATOUR, P. *Verités sur l'Afrique du Nord* (Paris,

1956). French Resident-General at Tunis and Rabat, 1954–5.

CAMUS, ALBERT. *Actuelles III: Chroniques algériennes, 1939–58* (Paris, 1958). Literary account of Algerian situation. See also Feraoun, Mouloud, *Journal, 1955–1962* (Paris, 1962).

AL-FASSI, ALLAL. *The Independence Movements in Arab North Africa* (Washington, 1954). Memoirs of Moroccan nationalist rather than a history.

GRANDVAL, GILBERT. *Ma Mission au Maroc* (Paris, 1956).

JUIN, GENERAL. *Le Maghreb en feu* (Paris, 1958). Very conservative French view of North African independence.

LYAUTEY, GENERAL H. L. (Later Marshal), *Paroles d'action* (Paris, 1938). French conquest of Morocco.

SFAR, TAHER. *Journal d'un exile* (Tunis, 1960). Member of Néo-Destour.

*SOUSTELLE, JACQUES. *Aimée et souffrante Algérie* (Paris, 1956).

3. GENERAL BOOKS ON BRITISH AND FRENCH POLICY

There are three perceptive studies on British policy in the area. The first two are short introductions to the subject, the third a full-length study.

BULLARD, SIR READER. *Britain and the Middle East* (3rd rev. ed., London, 1964).

HOURANI, A. H. *Great Britain and the Arab World* (London, 1945).

MONROE, ELIZABETH. *Britain's Moment in the Middle East, 1914–1956* (London, 1963).

There are no comparable studies of French policy in the area but material can be found in the following works.

CHASTENET, JACQUES. *Histoire de la troisième république* (Paris, 1952—). To be completed in seven volumes.

ROBERTS, STEPHEN H. *The History of French Colonial Policy 1870–1925* (London, 1925 and 1929). Reprinted in one-volume edition, 1963).

4. IMPERIALISM

The following section contains books on the principles underlying British and French imperial policy. They also put Mediterranean and Middle Eastern colonial experience into the larger perspective of the colonial empires.

BRUNSCHWIG, H. *French Colonialism 1871–1914: Myths and Realities* (London, 1966). Expanded version of the French edition.

DESCHAMPS, HUBERT. *Les Méthodes et les Doctrines coloniales de la France du XVIᵉ Siècle à nos Jours* (Paris, 1953).

FIELDHOUSE, D. K. 'Imperialism: an historiographical revision' in *Economic History Review*, 2nd series, vol. xiv (1962), pp. 187–209.

GRIMAL, HENRI. *La Décolonisation, 1919–1963* (Paris, 1965).

HOSKINS, H. L. *British Routes to India* (London, 1928).

ROBINSON, R. and GALLAGHER, J. *Africa and the Victorians: the Official Mind of Imperialism* (London, 1961).

THORNTON, A. P. *The Imperial Idea and its Enemies* (London, 1963).

The rest of the bibliography is divided into sections which illustrate the problems raised in the text of the book, and also present other facets of modern Middle Eastern political, social and economic history, and the relations of other Western powers with the area.

The Middle East and North Africa

The following books deal with social and economic change in the area.

BERGER, MONROE. *The Arab World Today* (New York, 1962).

BERQUE, JACQUES. *The Arabs: their History and Future* (London, 1964). (Translation of *Les Arabes d'hier à demain*, Paris, 1960.)

COON, CARLETON. *Caravan: the Story of the Middle East* (London, 1952).

FISHER, S. N. (ed.). *Social Forces in the Middle East* (Ithaca, New York, 1955).

HALPERN, MANFRED. *The Politics of Social Change in the Middle East and North Africa* (Princeton, 1963).

HERSHLAG, Z. Y. *Introduction to the Modern Economic History of the Middle East* (Leiden, 1964).

Individual studies of communities are now appearing in large numbers. The works of Jacques Berque, Roger le Tourneau and Robert Montagne on N. Africa are particularly to be recommended. E. E. Evans-Pritchard in Britain has written and inspired writing on social anthropology in the area.

The First World War in the Middle East (military history)

BRÉMOND, E. *Le Hedjaz dans la Guerre mondiale* (Paris, 1931).

EVANS, R. A. *Brief Outline of the Campaigns in Mesopotamia* (London, 1926).

GARDNER, BRIAN. *Allenby* (London, 1965).

JAMES, ROBERT RHODES. *Gallipoli* (London, 1965). A good study of this controversial episode.

LARCHER, M. *La Guerre turque dans la Guerre mondiale* (Paris, 1926).

Diplomacy in War and Peace

*CUMMING, HENRY H. *Franco-British Rivalry in the Post-War Near East* (London, 1938). Useful for its quotations from documents and letters.

GELFAND, LAWRENCE E. *The Inquiry: American Preparations for Peace, 1917–1919* (New Haven, 1963). Discusses American attitudes to the partition of the Ottoman Empire.

GOTTLIEB, W. W. *Studies in Secret Diplomacy during the First World War* (London, 1957). Background to the arrangements made for the Ottoman Empire.

HOWARD, HARRY N. *The King–Crane Commission: an American Inquiry into the Middle East* (Beirut, 1963). A detailed account of the terms of reference and findings of the commission.

HOWARD, HARRY N. *The Partition of Turkey: a Diplomatic History, 1913–1923* (Oklahoma, 1931). A thorough survey of the problem.

KEDOURIE, ELIE. *England and the Middle East: the destruction of the Ottoman Empire, 1914–1921* (London, 1956). Covers Arab opinion well.

LYAUTEY, PIERRE. *Le Drame oriental et le Rôle de la France* (Paris, 1923).

NICOLSON, SIR HAROLD. *Curzon: the Last Phase* (London, 1934) and *Peacemaking 1919* (London, 1933). Interesting for background comment on Peace Conference.

PINGAUD, A. *Histoire diplomatique de la France pendant la Grande Guerre.* Vols i and iii relevant (Paris, 1940). Explains French aims and ambitions.

STEIN, LEONARD. *The Balfour Declaration* (London, 1961). An excellent study of the events leading to the Declaration.

WEISGAL, M. and CARMICHAEL, J. (eds), *Chaim Weizmann: a biography by several hands* (London, 1962). Collection of essays on all aspects of Weizmann's career.

YALE, WILLIAM. 'Morgenthau's Special Mission of 1917', in *World Politics*, no. i (1949), pp. 308–26.

*ZEINE, Z. N. *The Struggle for Arab Independence: Western Diplomacy and the Rise and Fall of Feisal's Kingdom in Syria* (Beirut, 1960). A well-documented account of Arab aims.

The Lawrence Myth

The Seven Pillars of Wisdom (numerous editions) and *The Letters*, ed. David Garnett (London, 1938).

HART, B. LIDDELL. *Lawrence in Arabia and After* (London, 1934).

MOUSA, SULEIMAN. *T. E. Lawrence: an Arab View* (London, 1966).

PHILBY, H. ST. J. 'T. E. Lawrence and his critics', in *Forty Years in the Wilderness* (London, 1957).

VILLARS, JEAN BERAUD. *T. E. Lawrence* (London, 1955).

Turkey

The following books contain the best surveys of modern Turkey.

KINROSS, LORD. *Atatürk* (London, 1964).

LEWIS, B. *The Emergence of Modern Turkey* (London, 1961).

LEWIS, G. *Turkey* (3rd rev. ed., London, 1965).

On the Idea of Mandate

LOUIS, WILLIAM ROGER. 'Great Britain and international trusteeship; the Mandate System', in R. Winks (ed.), *The Historiography of the British Empire–Commonwealth* (Durham, N.C., 1966).

The Palestine Mandate

BENTWICH, NORMAN. *England in Palestine* (London, 1932). Jewish view of the British Mandate.

E.S.C.O. Foundation. *Palestine: a Study of Jewish, Arab and British Policies* (New Haven, Conn., 1947). Very full, documented account by number of authors.

HUREWITZ, J. C. *The Struggle for Palestine* (New York, 1950).

MARLOWE, J. *The Seat of Pilate* (London, 1959). General account of the Mandate.

HANNA, P. S. *British Policy in Palestine* (Washington, 1942).

R.I.I.A. *Great Britain and Palestine*, Information Papers, no. 20 (3rd. ed., London, 1946). Good short guide to the subject.

SYKES, CHRISTOPHER. *Crossroads to Israel* (London, 1965). Most balanced general survey of the Mandate.

Jordan

There is no satisfactory history of Jordan. The following are the best books available.

DEARDEN, ANN. *Jordan* (London, 1958).

GLUBB, J. BAGOT. *The Story of the Arab Legion* (London, 1946).

KIRKBRIDE, SIR ALEC. 'The National Government of Moab', in *A Crackle of Thorns* (London, 1956).

VATIKIOTIS, P. J. *Politics and the Military in Jordan: a Study of the Arab Legion, 1921–1957* (London, 1967).

The French Mandate in Syria and Lebanon

*HOURANI, A. H. *Syria and Lebanon: a Political Essay* (London, 1946). The best interpretation of the French Mandate.

LONGRIGG, S. H. *Syria and Lebanon under French Mandate* (London, 1958). A more factual account of the Mandate.

RABBATH, E. *Unité Syrienne et Devenir arabe* (Paris, 1937). Important for nationalist opinion.

RONDOT, PIERRE. *Les Chrétiens d'Orient* (Paris, 1955).

RONDOT, PIERRE. *Les Institutions politiques de Liban* (Paris, 1947).

SALIBI, KAMAL S. *The Modern History of Lebanon* (London, 1965).

ZIADEH, NICOLA A. *Syria and Lebanon* (London, 1957). Two rather thin and disappointing Arab accounts of the period.

Egypt and the Sudan

ABBAS, MEKKI. *The Sudan Question* (London, 1952). An Arab view of the problem.

COLLINS, ROBERT O. 'Egypt and the Sudan', in R. Winks (ed.). *The Historiography of the British Empire–Commonwealth* (Durham, N.C., 1966). Critical bibliographical survey.

COLLINS, ROBERT O., and TIGNOR, ROBERT L. *Egypt and the Sudan* (Englewood Cliffs, New Jersey, 1967). Good short introduction to the subject.

FABUNMI, L. A. *The Sudan in Anglo-Egyptian Relations, 1800–1956* (London, 1960). A solid account with documentary quotation.

HOLT, P. M. *A Modern History of the Sudan from the Funj Sultanate to the Present Day* (London, 1961).

KEDOURIE, ELIE. 'Sa'ad Zaghlul and the British', in *St Antony's Papers*, Middle Eastern Affairs, no. 2 (London, 1961), pp. 139–60.

LITTLE, TOM. *Egypt* (rev. ed., London, 1967). General history.

LLOYD, LORD. *Egypt since Cromer* (2 vols, London, 1933–4).

MACMICHAEL, SIR HAROLD. *The Sudan* (London, 1954). These two books are by British administrators in the countries.

MARLOWE, JOHN. *Anglo-Egyptian Relations, 1800–1953* (London, 1954). A general survey.

Iraq

The following books cover the political history of Iraq.

IRELAND, PHILIP W. *Iraq* (London, 1937).

KHADDURI, MAJID. *Independent Iraq: a Study in Iraqi politics from 1932 to 1958* (2nd ed., London, 1960).

LONGRIGG, S. H. *Iraq, 1900–1950* (London, 1953).

LONGRIGG, S. H. and STOAKES, FRANK. *Iraq* (London, 1958).

Iran, the Gulf and S. Arabia

AVERY, PETER. *Modern Iran* (London, 1965). Good political history.

HICKINBOTHAM, SIR TOM. *Aden* (London, 1958).

INGRAMS, HAROLD. *Arabia and the Isles* (3rd ed., London, 1966). Both these books are by British administrators in the area.

KELLY, J. B. *Eastern Arabian Frontiers* (London, 1964).

KELLY, J. B. 'The legal and historical basis of the British position in the Persian Gulf', in *St Antony's Papers*, Middle Eastern Affairs, 1 (London, 1958).

KELLY, J. B. *Sultanate and Imamate in Oman*, Chatham House Memorandum (London, 1959).

WILSON, SIR ARNOLD. *The Persian Gulf* (London, 1928). Origins of British commitments in the area.

Oil

ELWELL, SUTTON L. P. *Persian Oil: a Study in Power Politics* (London, 1955).

FORD, ALAN W. *The Anglo-Iranian Oil Dispute of 1951–1952* (Berkeley, California, 1954).

HARTSHORN, J. E. *Oil Companies and Governments* (2nd ed., London, 1966).

LEEMAN, W. A. *The Price of Middle East Oil* (Ithaca, N.Y., 1961).

LENCZOWSKI, G. *Oil and State in the Middle East* (Ithaca, N.Y., 1960).

LONGRIGG, S. H. *Oil in the Middle East* (3rd ed., London, 1968).

SHWADRAN, B. *The Middle East, Oil and the Great Powers* (2nd rev. ed., New York, 1959).

Resistance Movements in the Middle East

AHMED, J. M. *The Intellectual Origins of Egyptian Nationalism* (London, 1960).

ANTONIUS, GEORGE. *The Arab Awakening: the Story of the Arab National Movement* (London, 1938).

GIBB, SIR H. A. R. 'The Islamic Congress at Jerusalem in December, 1931', in *Survey of International Affairs*, 1934.

GIBB, SIR H. A. R. *Modern Trends in Islam* (Chicago, 1947).

*HAIM, SYLVIA (ed.). *Arab Nationalism: An Anthology* (Berkeley and Los Angeles, 1964).

HARRIS, CHRISTINE PHELPS. *Nationalism and Revolution in Egypt: the Role of the Muslim Brotherhood* (The Hague, 1964).

HOURANI, ALBERT. *Arabic Thought in the Liberal Age* (London, 1962).

KOESTLER, A. *Promise and Fulfilment: Palestine 1917-1949* (London, 1949).

LAMBTON, ANN K. S. 'The Impact of the West on Persia', in *International Affairs*, vol. 33 (1957).

LAQUEUR, WALTER Z. *Communism and Nationalism in the Middle East* (London, 1956).

LAQUEUR, WALTER Z. (ed.). *The Middle East in Transition* (London, 1958).

SAYEGH, FAYEZ A. *Arab Unity: Hope and Fulfilment* (New York, 1958).

SHARABI, HISHAM B. *Nationalism and Revolution in the Arab World, the Middle East and North Africa* (Princeton, N.J., 1966).

TAYLOR, ALAN R. *Prelude to Israel: an Analysis of Zionist Diplomacy* (New York, 1959).

ZEINE, ZEINE N. *Arab-Turkish Relations and the Emergence of Arab Nationalism* (Beirut, 1958).

Second World War

KIRK, G. E. *The Middle East in the War, 1939-1946* (London, 1952).

176   BIBLIOGRAPHY

PLAYFAIR, I. S. O. *The Mediterranean and the Middle East* (UK History of the Second World War, 4 vols in progress 1954—).

Israel

There is no completely satisfactory history of Israel.

BAR-ZOHAR, MICHEL. *Ben Gourion: prophète armé* (Paris, 1966). Uses Ben Gurion's papers.

BENTWICH, NORMAN. *Israel* (London, 1952).

EYTAN, WALTER. *The First Ten Years. Israel between East and West* (London, 1958).

FRIEDMANN, GEORGES. *Fin du peuple juif?* (Paris, 1965). (English trans., 1967.) Also reviews of this book in *Annales*, vol. 21, 1966. Interesting study of Israel's changing society.

SACHER, HARRY. *Israel: the Establishment of a State* (London, 1952).

Nasser's Egypt

CREMEANS, CHARLES D. *The Arabs and the World: Nasser's Arab Nationalist Policy* (New York, 1962). Puts Nasser's policy in wider Arab context.

KERR, MALCOLM. *Egypt under Nasser* (Headline series, no. 161 of American Foreign Policy Association, New York, 1963). Very good introductory essay.

MANSFIELD, PETER. *Nasser's Egypt* (London, 1965). Good short survey.

O'BRIEN, PATRICK. *The Revolution in Egypt's Economic System: from Private Enterprise to Socialism, 1952–1965* (Oxford, 1966).

SAAB, GABRIEL S. *The Egyptian Agrarian Reform, 1952–1962* (London, 1967). Two valuable economic studies.

WHEELOCK, K. *Nasser's New Egypt* (New York, 1960).

North Africa

BARBOUR, NEVILL (ed.). *A Survey of North-West Africa (The Maghrib)* (2nd ed., London, 1962). Reference book.

BERQUE, JACQUES. *Le Maghreb entre deux Guerres* (Paris, 1962). Perceptive interpretation of the period.

BRACE, RICHARD M. *Morocco, Algeria, Tunisia* (Englewood Cliffs, N.J., 1964). Short introduction to area.

DESPOIS, JEAN. *L'Afrique du nord* (2nd ed., Paris, 1960). A human geography of the area.

GALLAGHER, CHARLES F. *The United States and North Africa: Morocco, Algeria and Tunisia* (Cambridge, Mass., 1963). Of wider reference than the title suggests.

JULIEN, CHARLES-ANDRÉ. *L'Afrique du Nord en marche* (Paris, 1953). Sympathetic account of nationalist movement by French administrator.

LACOUTURE, JEAN. *Cinq Hommes et la France* (Paris, 1961). Contains essays on Ferhat Abbas, Bourguiba and Mohammed V.

LE TOURNEAU, ROGER. *Évolution politique de l'Afrique du Nord musulmane* (Paris, 1962). The best account of the independence movements.

MONROE, ELIZABETH. *The Mediterranean in Politics* (London, 1938). Good on problems of area in 1930s.

PEYROUTON, M. *Histoire générale du Maghreb* (Paris, 1966).

ZARTMAN, I. WILLIAM. *Government and Politics in Northern Africa* (New York, 1963). Also has sections on Egypt and Sudan.

Algeria

ESQUER, GABRIEL. *Histoire de L'Algérie, 1830–1960* (Que sais-je? series, Paris, 1960).

GAUTIER, E. F. *L'Évolution de l'Algérie de 1830 à 1930* (Algiers, 1931). The classic justification of French rule.

GORDON, DAVID C. *The Passing of French Algeria* (London, 1966). A good general survey.

LACOSTE, YVES and others. *L'Algérie passé et présent: le Cadre et les Étapes de la Constitution de l'Algérie actuelle* (Paris, 1960).

MINER, HORACE M. and VOS, GEORGE DE. *Oasis and Casbah: Algerian Culture and Personality in Change* (Ann Arbor, Michigan, 1960).

MORISOT, JEAN. *L'Algérie Kabylisée* (Paris, 1962). Sociological study of the area.

NOUSCHI, ANDRÉ. *La Naissance du Nationalisme algérien* (Paris, 1962). Well-documented left-wing account.

Morocco

AYACHE, A. *Le Maroc: Bilan d'une Colonisation* (Paris, 1956).

BARBOUR, NEVILL. *Morocco* (London, 1965).
Two general introductions.

CATROUX, GEORGES. *Lyautey le Marocain* (Paris, 1952).

MAXWELL, GAVIN. *Lords of the Atlas: the Rise and Fall of the House of Glaoua 1893–1958* (London, 1966).

MIÈGE, J-L. *Le Maroc* (Que sais-je? series, Paris, 1950).

MONTAGNE, ROBERT. *Les Berbères et le Makhzen dans le Sud du Maroc* (Paris, 1930).

MONTAGNE, ROBERT. *Naissance du Prolétariat Marocain* (Paris, 1950).

REZETTE, ROBERT. *Les Partis politiques Marocains* (Paris, 1955). Detailed study.

STEWART, C. F. *The Economy of Morocco 1912–1962* (Cambridge, Mass., 1964).

TÉRASSE, HENRI. *Initiation au Maroc* (Paris, 1945).

Tunisia

BASSET, A. and others. *Initiation à la Tunisie* (Paris, 1950).

DEMEERSEMAN, ANDRÉ. *Tunisie, Terre d'Amitié* (Tunis, 1955).

GARAS, FÉLIX. *Bourguiba et la Naissance d'une Nation* (Paris, 1956). Popular biography.

RAYMOND, ANDRÉ. *La Tunisie* (Que sais-je? series, Paris, 1961). Good short summary.

ROMERIL, PAUL E. A. 'Tunisian nationalism: a bibliographical outline', in *Middle East Journal*, vol. xiv (1960).

SEBAG, PAUL. *La Tunisie* (Paris, 1951).

TLATLI, SALAHEDDINE. *Tunisie nouvelle* (Tunis, 1957). A Tunisian account.

The Algerian Revolution

The Revolution produced much partisan literature. Where an extreme viewpoint is put forward this will be indicated in the following list.

General studies

ALWAN, MOHAMED. *Algeria before the United Nations* (New York, 1959).

BEHR, EDWARD. *The Algerian Problem* (London, 1961). Short introductory work.

BROMBERGER, SERGE. *Les Rebelles Algériens* (Paris, 1960).

BOURDIEU, PIERRE. *The Algerians* (Boston, 1962).

CLARK, MICHAEL K. *Algeria in Turmoil: a History of the Rebellion* (New York, 1959). Pro-French Algeria.

DUCHEMIN, JACQUES. *Histoire du F.L.N.* (Paris, 1962).

GILLESPIE, JOAN. *Algeria: Rebellion and Revolution* (London, 1960). Disappointing general account.

JEANSON, COLETTE and FRANCIS. *L'Algérie hors la Loi* (Paris, 1955). Pro FLN.

JEANSON, FRANCIS. *La Révolution Algérienne* (Milan, 1962).

LA NEF. *Histoire de la Guerre d'Algérie Suivie d'une Histoire de l'O.A.S.* (Cahier 12–13, Paris, Oct 1962–Jan 1963).

LOESCH, ANNE. *La Valise et le Cercueil* (Paris, 1963). Moderate *colon* view.

NORA, PIERRE. *Les Français d'Algérie* (Paris, 1961).

PICKLES, DOROTHY. *Algeria and France: from Colonialism to Co-operation* (London, 1963). Good introduction to the subject.

TILLION, GERMAINE. *Algeria: the Realities* (London, 1958).

VIDAL-NAQUET, PIERRE. *Torture: Cancer of Democracy: France and Algeria, 1954–1962* (London, 1963).

A number of books influenced French opinion in the course of the revolt; of these see Raymond Aron, *La Tragédie Algérienne* (Paris, 1957); Henri Alleg, *The Question* (trans. London, 1958) an account of the author's torture; J.-J. Servan-Schreiber, *Lieutenant en Algérie* (Paris, 1956) an account of army methods by editor of *L'Express*. Simone Beauvoir took up the case of Djamila Boupacha and with Gisèle Halimi wrote *Djamila Boupacha* (trans. London, 1962). The effect of France on Algerian intellectual life is dealt with in David C. Gordon, *North Africa's French Legacy: 1954–1962* (Cambridge, Mass., 1962).

North Africa gains Independence

ASHFORD, D. E. *Political Change in Morocco* (Princeton, 1961).

*BERNARD, STEPHANE. *Le Conflit franco-marocain 1943–1956* (3 vols, Brussels, 1963). Very full, well-documented account.

BROWN, LEON CARL. *State and Society in Independent North Africa* (Washington, 1966).

GUEN, MONCEF. *La Tunisie indépendente, face à son Économie* (Paris, 1961).

HAHN, LORNA. *North Africa: Nationalism to Nationhood* (Washington, 1960). Covers the ground but with inaccuracies.

LACOUTURE, JEAN and SIMONNE. *Le Maroc à l'Épreuve* (Paris, 1958). Problems of contemporary Morocco.

MICAUD, C. A. *Tunisia: the Politics of Modernisation* (New York, 1964).

MOORE, C. A. *Tunisia since Independence: the Dynamics of One-Party Government* (Cambridge, 1966).

PERROUX, FRANÇOIS (ed.). *L'Algérie de Demain* (Paris, 1962).

ZARTMAN, I. WILLIAM. *Destiny of a Dynasty: the Search for Institutions in Morocco's Developing Society* (Columbia, 1964).

The Way to Suez

ABIDI, AH. H. *Jordan, a Political Study 1948–1957* (London, 1965).

BIRDWOOD LORD. *Nuri as-Said* (London, 1959).

CAMPBELL, JOHN C. *Defense of the Middle East* (2nd ed., New York, 1958).

CROSSMAN, R. H. *Palestine Mission* (London, 1946). Author's contemporary account of his mission.

IONIDES, MICHAEL. *Divide and Lose: the Arab Revolt, 1955–1958* (London, 1960).

KIMCHE, JON. *Seven Fallen Pillars* (2nd ed., 1953).

KIMCHE, JON and DAVID. *Both Sides of the Hill: Britain and the Palestine War* (London, 1960). Two general accounts of period from Jewish sources.

KIRK, GEORGE E. *The Middle East, 1945–1950* (London, 1954). Good survey.

LACOUTURE, JEAN and SIMONNE. *Egypt in Transition* (trans. with revisions, London, 1958).

MONROE, ELIZABETH. 'Mr Bevin's Arab Policy', in *St Antony's Papers*, Middle Eastern Affairs, 2 (London, 1961). A good analysis of the post-war years.

R.I.I.A. *British Interests in the Mediterranean and the Middle East* (London, 1958). Valuable for subject indicated by the title.

SEALE, PATRICK. *The Struggle for Syria: a Study of Post-war Arab Politics, 1945–1958* (London, 1965). A good guide through the complexities of Syrian politics.

The Suez Crisis

These books are discussed in an appendix to this book.

AZEAU, HENRI. *Le Piège de Suez* (Paris, 1964).

BAR-ZOHAR, MICHEL. *Suez Ultra Secret* (Paris, 1964).

FINER, HERMAN. *Dulles Over Suez: the Theory and Practice of his Diplomacy* (London, 1964).

HOURANI, ALBERT. 'The crisis of 1956', in *St Antony's Papers*, Middle Eastern Affairs, 1 (London, 1958).

MONCRIEFF, ANTHONY (ed.). *Suez Ten Years After* (London, 1967).

MONROE, ELIZABETH. 'Suez secrets', in the *Observer* (24 July 1966).

NUTTING, ANTHONY. *No End of a Lesson: the Story of Suez* (London, 1967).

ROBERTSON, TERENCE. *Crisis: the Inside Story of the Suez Conspiracy* (London, 1965).

THOMAS, HUGH. *The Suez Affair* (London, 1967).

WATT, D. C. *Britain and the Suez Canal: the Background* (London, 1956).

The Decade 1956–66

HOLDEN, DAVID. *Farewell to Arabia* (London, 1966). Sound and readable account of S. Arabian problem.

INGRAMS, HAROLD. *Arabia and the Isles* (3rd ed., London, 1966).

KERR, MALCOLM. 'Coming to terms with Nasser', in *International Affairs* (January, 1967). American attitudes towards Nasser, but also indicates Nasser's difficulties.

KERR, MALCOLM. *The Arab Cold War, 1958–1964: a Study of Ideology in Politics*, Chatham House essays, 10 (London, 1965). Sheds light on problems of Arab co-operation.

KING, GILLIAN. *Imperial Outpost – Aden: its Place in British Strategic Policy*, Chatham House essays, 6 (London, 1964). Good summary of British commitments.

MONROE, ELIZABETH. 'The Middle East', in Evan Luard (ed.), *The Cold War* (London, 1964). The post-war Middle East in the eyes of the Western powers.

QUBAIN, FAHIM. *Crisis in Lebanon* (Washington, 1961).

RONDOT, PIERRE. *Changing Patterns of the Middle East, 1919–1958* (trans. London, 1961). Survey of Middle East from viewpoint of 1958.

SARNE, DANIEL. *L'Affaire Ben Barka* (Paris, 1966). The best summary to date of this unfathomable affair.

STEVENS, GEORGIANA G. *Jordan River Partition*, Hoover Institution Studies (Stanford, 1965). Good summary of the problems.

Other Powers in the Area

DE NOVO, JOHN A. *American Interests and Policies in the Middle East, 1900–1939* (Minneapolis, 1963).

GALLAGHER, CHARLES A. *The United States and North Africa* (Cambridge, Mass., 1963).

HIRSZOWICZ, LUKASZ. *The Third Reich and the Arab East* (London, 1966).

LAQUEUR, W. Z. *The Soviet Union and the Middle East* (New York, 1959).

LENCZOWSKI, GEORGE. *Russia and the West in Iran 1918–1948: a Study in Big-Power Rivalry* (Ithaca, N.Y., 1949).

MANUEL, FRANK E. *The Realities of American-Palestine Relations* (Washington, 1949).

NOLLAU, GÜNTHER and WIEHE, HANS JURGEN. *Russia's South Flank: Soviet Operations in Iran, Turkey and Afghanistan* (London, 1963).

POLK, W. R. *The United States and the Arab World* (Cambridge, Mass., 1965).

STEVENS, GEORGIANA G. (ed.). *The United States and the Middle East* (Englewood Cliffs, N.J., 1964).

WHEELER, GEOFFREY. 'Russia and the Middle East', in *International Affairs*, vol. 35 (1959).

Investment in the Middle East

HERSHLAG, Z. Y. *Introduction to the Modern Economic History of the Middle East* (Leiden, 1964).

DUCRUET, J. *Les Capitaux Européens au Proche-Orient* (Paris, 1964).

The World Bank has produced a number of surveys on the economies of various countries in the Middle East and North Africa, for example Syria and Morocco. Statistical publications of the United Nations and the individual countries of the area can be found in the specialist libraries listed below.

For Reference

BULLARD, SIR READER (ed.). *The Middle East: a Political and Economic Survey* (3rd ed., London, 1958). Political and economic summaries of countries in the area.

KINGSBURY, ROBERT C. and POUNDS, NORMAN J. G. *An Atlas of Middle Eastern Affairs* (London, 1964; reprint 1966). A disappointing survey of the region. The North African maps and comment are far better in Andrew Boyd and Patrick van Rensburg, *An Atlas of African Affairs* (London, first published in 1962, revised editions have appeared subsequently).

Europa Publications. *The Middle East and North Africa* (12 ed., 1965–6. Began publication in 1948, yearly since 1961). Information about countries of the area. Who's Who at the back.

The Israel Oriental Society produces the *Middle East Record* (London, 1960—), a year-book with similar information. *Keesing's Contemporary Archives* is also valuable.

Periodical Publications

Newspapers   *Le Monde* (Paris).
              The Guardian and *The Times* (London).
Daily   *B.B.C. Summary of World Broadcasts* (London,
              1939—). Separate section on Arab world
              since 1949.
Weeklies   *The Jewish Observer and Middle East Review*
              (London, 1952—).
              The Mid-East Mirror (London, 1949).
Quarterly   *Les Cahiers de l'Orient contemporain* (Paris,
              1945—).
              The Middle East Journal (Washington,
              1947—).
              Orient (Paris, 1957—).
              Oriente moderno (Rome, 1921—).

For Further Research

The libraries of the School of Oriental and African Studies,
University of London; the School of Oriental Studies,
University of Durham; and the Middle East Centre,
St Antony's College, Oxford, have specialist collections.
Durham also houses the papers of Sir Reginald Wingate
and is building a Sudan archive. St Antony's Middle East
Centre is collecting private papers on British rule in the
Middle East.

In France

Centre des Hautes Études sur l'Afrique et l'Asie modernes
(C.H.E.A.M.) in Paris (founded in 1936 under the title
Centre des Hautes Études d'Administration musulmane);
Centre d'Études Nord-Africains (C.E.N.A.) established
in Aix-en-Provence in 1958, and now called C.R.A.M.
(Centre de Recherches sur l'Afrique musulmane).

Index

Offices and titles are those held during the period covered by the book.